Shakespeare, Bacon, And The Great Unknown

Andrew Lang

Shakespeare, Bacon, and the Great Unknown

Copyright © 2020 Bibliotech Press
All rights reserved

The present edition is a reproduction of previous publication of this classic work. Minor typographical errors may have been corrected without note, however, for an authentic reading experience the spelling, punctuation, and capitalization have been retained from the original text.

ISBN: 978-1-64799-629-1

TO
HORACE HOWARD FURNESS
IN MEMORY OF AN
OLD PROMISE

CONTENTS

	Preface	v
	Introduction	vi
I	The Baconian and Anti-Willian Positions	1
II	The "Silence" about Shakespeare	13
III	That Impossible He—The Schooling of Shakespeare...	20
IV	Mr Collins on Shakespeare's Learning	33
V	Shakespeare, Genius, and Society	41
VI	The Courtly Plays: "Love's Labour's Lost"	58
VII	Contemporary Recognition of Will as Author	65
VIII	"The Silence of Philip Henslowe"	75
IX	The Later Life of Shakespeare—His Monument and Portraits	81
X	"The Traditional Shakspere"	93
XI	The First Folio	98
XII	Ben Jonson and Shakespeare	113
XIII	The Preoccupations of Bacon	132
	Appendix I—"Troilus and Cressida"	142
	Appendix II—Chettle's Supposed Allusion to Will Shakspere	147

PREFACE

It is with some hesitation that I give my husband's last book to the world. It was in type when he died, but he had no time to correct even the first proofs, and doubtless he would have made many changes, if not in his views at least in his expression of them. Mr. Bartram has verified the quotations and dates with infinite care, and for this he has my warmest thanks. For the rest I can but ask those who differ from the author to remember the circumstances in which the work has been published.

L. B. L.

INTRODUCTION

The theory that Francis Bacon was, in the main, the author of "Shakespeare's plays," has now been for fifty years before the learned world. Its advocates have met with less support than they had reason to expect. Their methods, their logic, and their hypotheses closely resemble those applied by many British and foreign scholars to Homer; and by critics of the very Highest School to Holy Writ. Yet the Baconian theory is universally rejected in England by the professors and historians of English literature; and generally by students who have no profession save that of Letters. The Baconians, however, do not lack the countenance and assistance of highly distinguished persons, whose names are famous where those of mere men of letters are unknown; and in circles where the title of "Professor" is not duly respected.

The partisans of Bacon aver (or one of them avers) that "Lord Penzance, Lord Beaconsfield, Lord Palmerston, Judge Webb, Judge Holmes (of Kentucky, U.S.), Prince Bismarck, John Bright, and innumerable most thoughtful scholars eminent in many walks of life, and especially in the legal profession..." have been Baconians, or, at least, opposed to Will Shakspere's authorship. To these names of scholars I must add that of my late friend, Samuel Clemens, D.Litt. of Oxford; better known to many as Mark Twain. Dr. Clemens was, indeed, no mean literary critic; witness his epoch-making study of Prof. Dowden's Life of Shelley, while his researches into the biography of Jeanne d'Arc were most conscientious.

With the deepest respect for the political wisdom and literary taste of Lord Palmerston, Prince Bismarck, Lord Beaconsfield, and the late Mr. John Bright; and with every desire to humble myself before the judicial verdicts of Judges Holmes, Webb, and Lord Penzance; with sincere admiration of my late friend, Dr. Clemens, I cannot regard them as, in the first place and professionally, trained students of literary history.

They were no more specially trained students of Elizabethan literature than myself; they were amateurs in this province, as I am an amateur, who differ from all of them in opinion. Difference of opinion concerning points of literary history ought not to make "our angry passions rise." Yet this controversy has been extremely bitter.

I abstain from quoting the "sweetmeats," in Captain MacTurk's phrase, which have been exchanged by the combatants. Charges of ignorance and monomania have been answered by charges of forgery, lying, "scandalous literary dishonesty," and even inaccuracy. Now no mortal is infallibly accurate, but we are all sane and "indifferent honest." There have been forgeries in matters Shakespearean, alas, but not in connection with the Baconian controversy.

It is an argument of the Baconians, and generally of the impugners of good Will's authorship of the plays vulgarly attributed to him, that the advocates of William Shakspere, Gent, as author of the plays, differ like the Kilkenny cats among themselves on many points. All do not believe, with Mr. J. C. Collins, that Will knew Sophocles, Euripides, and Æschylus (but not Aristophanes) as well as Mr. Swinburne did, or knew them at all—for that matter. Mr. Pollard differs very widely from Sir Sidney Lee on points concerning the First Folio and the Quartos: my sympathies are with Mr. Pollard. Few, if any, partisans of Will agree with Mrs. Stopes (herself no Baconian) about the history of the Stratford monument of the poet. About Will's authorship of Titus Andronicus, and Henry VI, Part I, the friends of Will, like the friends of Bacon, are at odds among themselves. These and other divergencies of opinion cause the Baconians to laugh, as if they were a harmonious circle ... ! For the Baconian camp is not less divided against itself than the camp of the "Stratfordians." Not all Baconians hold that Bacon was the legitimate son of "that Imperial votaress" Queen Elizabeth. Not all believe in the Cryptogram of Mr. Ignatius Donnelly, or in any other cryptograms. Not all maintain that Bacon, in the Sonnets, was inspired by a passion for the Earl of Essex, for Queen Elizabeth, or for an early miniature of himself. Not all regard him as the author of the plays of Kit Marlowe. Not all suppose him to be a Rosicrucian, who possibly died at the age of a hundred and six, or, perhaps, may be "still running." Not all aver that he wrote thirteen plays before 1593. But one party holds that, in the main, Will was the author of the plays, while the other party votes for Bacon—or for Bungay, a Great Unknown. I use Bungay as an endearing term for the mysterious being who was the Author if Francis Bacon was not. Friar Bungay was the rival of Friar Bacon, as the Unknown (if he was not Francis Bacon) is the rival of "the inventor of Inductive reasoning."

I could never have expected that I should take a part in this controversy; but acquaintance with The Shakespeare Problem Restated (503 pp.), (1908), and later works of Mr. G. G. Greenwood, M.P., has tempted me to enter the lists.

Mr. Greenwood is worth fighting; he is cunning of fence, is learned (and I cannot conceal my opinion that Mr. Donnelly and Judge Holmes were rather ignorant). He is not over "the threshold of Eld" (as were Judge Webb and Lord Penzance when they took up

Shakespearean criticism). His knowledge of Elizabethan literature is vastly superior to mine, for I speak merely, in Matthew Arnold's words, as "a belletristic trifler."

Moreover, Mr. Greenwood, as a practising barrister, is a judge of legal evidence; and, being a man of sense, does not "hold a brief for Bacon" as the author of the Shakespearean plays and poems, and does not value Baconian cryptograms. In the following chapters I make endeavours, conscientious if fallible, to state the theory of Mr. Greenwood. It is a negative theory. He denies that Will Shakspere (or Shaxbere, or Shagspur, and so on) was the author of the plays and poems. Some other party was, in the main, with other hands, the author. Mr. Greenwood cannot, or does not, offer a guess as to who this ingenious Somebody was. He does not affirm, and he does not deny, that Bacon had a share, greater or less, in the undertaking.

In my brief tractate I have not room to consider every argument; to traverse every field. In philology I am all unlearned, and cannot pretend to discuss the language of Shakespeare, any more than I can analyse the language of Homer into proto-Arcadian and Cyprian, and so on. Again, I cannot pretend to have an opinion, based on internal evidence, about the genuine Shakespearean character of such plays as Titus Andronicus, Henry VI, Part I, and Troilus and Cressida. About them different views are held within both camps.

I am no lawyer or naturalist (as Partridge said, Non omnia possumus omnes), and cannot imagine why our Author is so accurate in his frequent use of terms of law—if he be Will; and so totally at sea in natural history—if he be Francis, who "took all knowledge for his province."

How can a layman pretend to deal with Shakespeare's legal attainments, after he has read the work of the learned Recorder of Bristol, Mr. Castle, K.C.? To his legal mind it seems that in some of Will's plays he had the aid of an expert in law, and then his technicalities were correct. In other plays he had no such tutor, and then he was sadly to seek in his legal jargon. I understand Mr. Greenwood to disagree on this point. Mr. Castle says, "I think Shakespeare would have had no difficulty in getting aid from several sources. There is therefore no prima facie reason why we should suppose the information was supplied by Bacon."

Of course there is not!

"In fact, there are some reasons why one should attribute the legal assistance, say, to Coke, rather than to Bacon."

The truth is, that Bacon seems not to have been lawyer enough for Will's purposes. "We have no reason to believe that

Bacon was particularly well read in the technicalities of our law; he never seems to have seriously followed his profession."[1]

Now we have Mr. Greenwood's testimonial in favour of Mr. Castle, "Who really does know something about law."[2] Mr. Castle thinks that Bacon really did not know enough about law, and suggests Sir Edward Coke, of all human beings, as conceivably Will's "coach" on legal technicalities. Perhaps Will consulted the Archbishop of Canterbury on theological niceties?

Que sçais je? In some plays, says Mr. Castle, Will's law is all right, in other plays it is all wrong. As to Will's law, when Mr. Greenwood and Mr. Castle differ, a layman dare not intervene.

Concerning legend and tradition about our Will, it seems that, in each case, we should do our best to trace the Quellen, to discover the original sources, and the steps by which the tale arrived at its late recorders in print; and then each man's view as to the veracity of the story will rest on his sense of probability; and on his bias, his wish to believe or to disbelieve.

There exists, I believe, only one personal anecdote of Will, the actor, and on it the Baconians base an argument against the contemporary recognition of him as a dramatic author. I take the criticism of Mr. Greenwood (who is not a Baconian). One John Manningham, Barrister-at-Law, "a well-educated and cultured man," notes in his Diary (February 2, 1601) that "at our feast we had a play called Twelve Night or What you Will, much like the Comedy of Errors, or Menæchmi in Plautus, but most like and near to that in Italian called Inganni." He confides to his Diary the tricks played on Malvolio as "a good practice."[3] That is all.

About the authorship he says nothing: perhaps he neither knew nor cared who the author was. In our day the majority of people who tell me about a play which they have seen, cannot tell me the name of the author. Yet it is usually printed on the playbill, though in modest type. The public does not care a straw about the author's name, unless he be deservedly famous for writing letters to the newspapers on things in general; for his genius as an orator; his enthusiasm as a moralist, or in any other extraneous way. Dr. Forman in his queer account of the plot of "Mack Beth" does not allude to the name of the author (April 20, 1610). Twelfth Night was not published till 1623, in the Folio: there was no quarto to enlighten Manningham about the author's name. We do not hear of printed playbills, with author's names inserted, at that period. It

---

[1] E. J. Castle, Shakespeare, Bacon, Jonson, and Greene, pp. 194–195.
[2] The Shakespeare Problem Restated, p. 145.
[3] The Shakespeare Problem Restated, p. 340.

seems probable that occasional playgoers knew and cared no more about authors than they do at present. The world of the wits, the critics (such as Francis Meres), poets, playwrights, and players, did know and care about the authors; apparently Manningham did not. But he heard a piquant anecdote of two players and (March 13, 1601) inserted it in his Diary.

Shakespeare once anticipated Richard Burbage at an amorous tryst with a citizen's wife. Burbage had, by the way, been playing the part of Richard III. While Will was engaged in illicit dalliance, the message was brought (what a moment for bringing messages!) that Richard III was at the door, and Will "caused return to be made that William the Conqueror was before Richard III. Shakespeare's name William." (My italics.) Mr. Greenwood argues that if "Shakspere the player was known to the world as the author of the plays of Shakespeare, it does seem extremely remarkable" that Manningham should have thought it needful to add "Shakespeare's name William."[4]

But was "Shakspere," or any man, "known to the world as the author of the plays of Shakespeare"? No! for Mr. Greenwood writes, "nobody, outside a very small circle, troubled his head as to who the dramatist or dramatists might be."[5] To that "very small circle" we have no reason to suppose that Manningham belonged, despite his remarkable opinion that Twelfth Night resembles the Menæchmi. Consequently, it is not "extremely remarkable" that Manningham wrote "Shakespeare's name William," to explain to posterity the joke about "William the Conqueror," instead of saying, "the brilliant author of the Twelfth Night play which so much amused me at our feast a few weeks ago."[6] "Remarkable" out of all hooping it would have been had Manningham written in the style of Mr. Greenwood. But Manningham apparently did not "trouble his head as to who the dramatist or dramatists might be." "Nobody, outside a very small circle," did trouble his poor head about that point. Yet Mr. Greenwood thinks "it does seem extremely remarkable" that Manningham did not mention the author.

Later, on the publication of the Folio (1623), the world seems to have taken more interest in literary matters. Mr. Greenwood says that then while "the multitude" would take Ben Jonson's noble panegyric on Shakespeare as a poet "au pied de la lettre," "the enlightened few would recognise that it had an esoteric meaning."[7]

---

[4] The Shakespeare Problem Restated, pp. 340, 341.
[5] In Re Shakespeare, p. 54.
[6] The Shakespeare Problem Restated, p. 341.
[7] Ibid., p. 470.

Then, it seems, "the world"—the "multitude"—regarded the actor as the author. Only "the enlightened few" were aware that when Ben said "Shakespeare," and "Swan of Avon," he meant—somebody else.

Quite different inferences are drawn from the same facts by persons of different mental conditions. For example, in 1635 or 1636, Cuthbert Burbage, brother of Richard, the famous actor, Will's comrade, petitioned Lord Pembroke, then Lord Chamberlain, for consideration in a quarrel about certain theatres. Telling the history of the houses, he mentions that the Burbages "to ourselves joined those deserving men, Shakspere, Heminge, Condell, Phillips and others." Cuthbert is arguing his case solely from the point of the original owners or lease-holders of the houses, and of the well-known actors to whom they joined themselves. Judge Webb and Mr. Greenwood think that "it does indeed seem strange ... that the proprietor[s] of the playhouses which had been made famous by the production of the Shakespearean plays, should, in 1635—twelve years after the publication of the great Folio—describe their reputed author to the survivor of the Incomparable Pair, as merely a 'man-player' and 'a deserving man.'" Why did he not remind the Lord Chamberlain that this "deserving man" was the author of all these famous dramas? Was it because he was aware that the Earl of Pembroke "knew better than that"?[8]

These arguments are regarded by some Baconians as proof positive of their case.

Cuthbert Burbage, in 1635 or 1636, did not remind the Earl of what the Earl knew very well, that the Folio had been dedicated, in 1623, to him and his brother, by Will's friends, Heminge and Condell, as they had been patrons of the late William Shakspere and admirers of his plays. The terms of this dedication are to be cited in the text, later. We all now would have reminded the Earl of what he very well knew. Cuthbert did not.

The intelligence of Cuthbert Burbage may be gauged by anyone who will read pp. 481–484 in William Shakespeare, His Family and Friends, by the late Mr. Charles Elton, Q.C., of White Staunton. Cuthbert was a puzzle-pated old boy. The silence as to Will's authorship on the part of this muddle-headed old Cuthbert, in 1635–36, cannot outweigh the explicit and positive public testimony to his authorship, signed by his friends and fellow-actors in 1623.

Men believe what they may; but I prefer positive evidence for the affirmative to negative evidence from silence, the silence of Cuthbert Burbage.

One may read through Mr. Greenwood's three books and note

---

[8] The Shakespeare Problem Restated, p. 339.

the engaging varieties of his views; they vary as suits his argument; but he is unaware of it, or can justify his varyings. Thus, in 1610, one John Davies wrote rhymes in which he speaks of "our English Terence, Mr. Will Shakespeare"; "good Will." In his period patriotic English critics called a comic dramatist "the English Terence," or "the English Plautus," precisely as American critics used to call Mr. Bryant "the American Wordsworth," or Cooper "the American Scott"; and as Scots called the Rev. Mr. Thomson "the Scottish Turner." Somewhere, I believe, exists "the Belgian Shakespeare."

Following this practice, Davies had to call Will either "our English Terence," or "our English Plautus." Aristophanes would not have been generally recognised; and Will was no more like one of these ancient authors than another. Thus Davies was apt to choose either Plautus or Terence; it was even betting which he selected. But he chanced to choose Terence; and this is "curious," and suggests suspicions to Mr. Greenwood—and the Baconians. They are so very full of suspicions!

It does not suit the Baconians, or Mr. Greenwood, to find contemporary recognition of Will as an author.[9] Consequently, Mr. Greenwood finds Davies's "curious, and at first sight, inappropriate comparison of 'Shake-speare' to Terence worthy of remark, for Terence is the very author whose name is alleged to have been used as a mask-name, or nom de plume, for the writings of great men who wished to keep the fact of their authorship concealed."

Now Davies felt bound to bring in some Roman parallel to Shakespeare; and had only the choice of Terence or Plautus. Meres (1598) used Plautus; Davies used Terence. Mr. Greenwood[10] shows us that Plautus would not do. "Could he" (Shakespeare) "write only of courtesans and cocottes, and not of ladies highly born, cultured, and refined? ... "

"The supposed parallel" (Plautus and Shakespeare) "breaks down at every point." Thus, on Mr. Greenwood's showing, Plautus could not serve Davies, or should not serve him, in his search for a Roman parallel to "good Will." But Mr. Greenwood also writes, "if he" (Shakespeare) "was to be likened to a Latin comedian, surely Plautus is the writer with whom he should have been compared."[11] Yet Plautus was the very man who cannot be used as a parallel to Shakespeare. Of course no Roman nor any other comic dramatist closely resembles the author of As You Like It. They who selected either Plautus or Terence meant no more than that both were

---

[9] The Vindicators of Shakespeare, pp. 115–116.
[10] Ibid., p. 49.
[11] The Vindicators of Shakespeare, p. 14.

celebrated comic dramatists. Plautus was no parallel to Will. Yet "surely Plautus is the author to whom he should have been compared" by Davies, says Mr. Greenwood. If Davies tried Plautus, the comparison was bad; if Terence, it was "curious," as Terence was absurdly accused of being the "nom de plume" of some great "concealed poets" of Rome. "From all the known facts about Terence," says a Baconian critic (who has consulted Smith's Biographical Dictionary), "it is an almost unavoidable inference that John Davies made the comparison to Shakspere because he knew of the point common to both cases." The common point is taken to be, not that both men were famous comic dramatists, but that Roman literary gossips said, and that Baconians and Mr. Greenwood say, that "Terence" was said to be a "mask-name," and that "Shakespeare" is a mask-name. Of the second opinion there is not a hint in literature of the time of good Will.

What surprises one most in this controversy is that men eminent in the legal profession should be "anti-Shakesperean," if not overtly Baconian. For the evidence for the contemporary faith in Will's authorship is all positive; from his own age comes not a whisper of doubt, not even a murmur of surprise. It is incredible to me that his fellow-actors and fellow-playwrights should have been deceived, especially when they were such men as Ben Jonson and Tom Heywood. One would expect lawyers, of all people, to have been most impatient of the surprising attempts made to explain away Ben Jonson's testimony, by aid, first, of quite a false analogy (Scott's denial of his own authorship of his novels), and, secondly, by the suppression of such a familiar fact as the constant inconsistency of Ben's judgments of his contemporaries in literature. Mr. Greenwood must have forgotten the many examples of this inconsistency; but I have met a Baconian author who knew nothing of the fact. Mr. Greenwood, it is proper to say, does not seem to be satisfied that he has solved what he calls "the Jonsonian riddle." Really, there is no riddle. About Will, as about other authors, his contemporaries and even his friends, on occasion, Ben "spoke with two voices," now in terms of hyperbolical praise, now in carping tones of censure. That is the obvious solution of "the Jonsonian riddle."

I must apologise if I have in places spelled the name of the Swan of Avon "Shakespeare" where Mr. Greenwood would write "Shakspere," and vice versa. He uses "Shakespeare" where he means the Author; "Shakspere" where he means Will; and is vexed with some people who write the name of Will as "Shakespeare." As Will, in the opinion of a considerable portion of the human race, and of myself, was the Author, one is apt to write his name as

"Shakespeare" in the usual way. But difficult cases occur, as in quotations, and in conditional sentences. By any spelling of the name I always mean the undivided personality of "Him who sleeps by Avon."

I
THE BACONIAN AND ANTI-WILLIAN POSITIONS

Till the years 1856–7 no voice was raised against the current belief about Shakespeare (1564–1616). He was the author in the main of the plays usually printed as his. In some cases other authors, one or more, may have had fingers in his dramas; in other cases, Shakespeare may have "written over" and transfigured earlier plays, of himself and of others; he may have contributed, more or less, to several plays mainly by other men. Separately printed dramas published during his time carry his name on their title-pages, but are not included in the first collected edition of his dramas, "The First Folio," put forth by two of his friends and fellow-actors, in 1623, seven years after his death.

On all these matters did commentators, critics, and antiquarians for long dispute; but none denied that the actor, Will Shakspere (spelled as heaven pleased), was in the main the author of most of the plays of 1623, and the sole author of Venus and Adonis, Lucrece, and the Sonnets.

Even now, in England at least, it would be perhaps impossible to find one special and professed student of Elizabethan literature, and of the classical and European literatures, who does not hold by the ancient belief, the belief of Shakespeare's contemporaries and intimates, the belief that he was, in the sense explained above, the author of the plays.

But ours is not a generation to be overawed by "Authority" (as it is called). A small but eager company of scholars have convinced themselves that Francis Bacon wrote the Shakespearean plays. That is the point of agreement among these enthusiasts: points of difference are numerous: some very wild little sects exist. Meanwhile multitudes of earnest and intelligent men and women, having read notices in newspapers of the Baconian books, or heard of them at lectures and tea-parties, disbelieve in the authorship of "the Stratford rustic," and look down on the faithful of Will Shakespere with extreme contempt.

From the Baconians we receive a plain straightforward theory, "Bacon wrote Shakespeare," as one of their own prophets has said.[12] Since we have plenty of evidence for Bacon's life and occupations

---

[12] Francis Bacon Wrote Shakespeare. By H. Crouch-Batchelor, 1912.

during the period of Shakespearean poetic activity, we can compare what he was doing as a man, a student, a Crown lawyer, a pleader in the Courts, a political pamphleteer, essayist, courtier, active member of Parliament, and so on, with what he is said to have been doing—by the Baconians; namely, writing two dramas yearly.

But there is another "Anti-Willian" theory, which would dethrone Will Shakspere, and put but a Shadow in his place. Conceive a "concealed poet," of high social position, contemporary with Bacon and Shakespeare. Let him be so fond of the Law that he cannot keep legal "shop" out of his love Sonnets even. Make him a courtier; a statesman; a philosopher; a scholar who does not blench even from the difficult Latin of Ovid and Plautus. Let this almost omniscient being possess supreme poetic genius, extensive classical attainments, and a tendency to make false quantities. Then conceive him to live through the reigns of "Eliza and our James," without leaving in history, in science, in society, in law, in politics or scholarship, a single trace of his existence. He left nothing but the poems and plays usually attributed to Will. As to the date of his decease, we only know that it must necessarily have been later than the composition of the last genuine Shakespearean play—for this paragon wrote it.

Such is the Being who occupies, in the theory of the non-Baconian, but not Anti-Baconian, Anti-Willians, the intellectual throne filled, in the Will Shakespeare theory, by Will; and in the Baconian, by Bacon—two kings of Brentford on one throne.

We are to be much engaged by the form of this theory which is held by Mr. G. G. Greenwood in his The Shakespeare Problem Restated. In attempting to explain what he means I feel that I am skating on very thin ice. Already, in two volumes (In Re Shakespeare, 1909, and The Vindicators of Shakespeare), Mr. Greenwood has accused his critics of frequently misconceiving and misrepresenting his ideas: wherefore I also tremble. I am perfectly confident in saying that he "holds no brief for the Baconians." He is not a Baconian. His position is negative merely: Will of Stratford is not the author of the Shakespearean plays and poems. Then who is? Mr. Greenwood believes that work by an unknown number of hands exists in the plays first published all together in 1623. Here few will differ from him. But, setting aside this aspect of the case, Mr. Greenwood appears to me to believe in an entity named "Shakespeare," or "the Author," who is the predominating partner; though Mr. Greenwood does not credit him with all the plays in the Folio of 1623 (nor, perhaps, with the absolute entirety of any given play). "The Author" or "Shakespeare" is not a syndicate (like the Homer of many critics), but an individual human being, apparently of the male sex. As to the name by which he was called on earth, Mr. Greenwood is "agnostic." He himself is not Anti-Baconian. He does not oust Bacon and put the Unknown in his place. He neither affirms nor denies that Bacon may have contributed, more or less, to the bulk of Shakespearean work. To put it briefly: Mr. Greenwood backs the field against the favourite (our Will), and Bacon may be in the field. If he has any part in the whole I suspect that it is "the lion's part," but Mr. Greenwood does not commit himself to anything positive. We shall find (if I am not mistaken) that Mr. Greenwood regards the hypothesis of the Baconians as "an extremely reasonable one,"[13] and that for his purposes it would be an extremely serviceable one, if not even essential. For as Bacon was a genius to whose potentialities one can set no limit, he is something to stand by, whereas we cannot easily believe—I cannot believe—that the actual "Author," the "Shakespeare" lived and died and left no trace of his existence except his share in the works called Shakespearean.

However, the idea of the Great Unknown has, for its partisans, this advantage, that as the life of the august Shade is wholly unknown, we cannot, as in Bacon's case, show how he was occupied while the plays were being composed. He must, however, have been much at Court, we learn, and deep in the mysteries of legal terminology. Was he Sir Edward Coke? Was he James VI and I?

It is hard, indeed, to set forth the views of the Baconians and of the "Anti-Willians" in a shape which will satisfy them. The task, especially when undertaken by an unsympathetic person, is perhaps impossible. I can only summarise their views in my own words as far as I presume to understand them. I conceive the Baconians to cry that "the world possesses a mass of transcendent literature, attributed to a man named William Shakespeare." Of a man named William Shakspere (there are many varieties of spelling) we certainly know that he was born (1564) and bred in Stratford-on-Avon, a peculiarly dirty, stagnant, and ignorant country town. There is absolutely no evidence that he (or any Stratford boy of his standing) ever went to Stratford school. His father, his mother, and his daughter could not write, but, in signing, made their marks; and if he could write, which some of us deny, he wrote a terribly bad hand. As far as late traditions of seventy or eighty years after his death inform us, he was a butcher's apprentice; and also a schoolmaster "who knew Latin pretty well"; and a poacher. He made, before he was nineteen, a marriage tainted with what Meg Dods calls "ante-nup." He early had three children, whom he

---

[13] The Shakespere Problem Restated, p. 293.

deserted, as he deserted his wife. He came to London, we do not know when (about 1582, according to the "guess" of an antiquary of 1680); held horses at the door of a theatre (so tradition says), was promoted to the rank of "servitor" (whatever that may mean), became an actor (a vagabond under the Act), and by 1594 played before Queen Elizabeth. He put money in his pocket (heaven knows how), for by 1597 he was bargaining for the best house in his native bourgade. He obtained, by nefarious genealogical falsehoods (too common, alas, in heraldry), the right to bear arms; and went on acting. In 1610–11 (?) he retired to his native place. He never took any interest in his unprinted manuscript plays; though rapacious, he never troubled himself about his valuable copyrights; never dreamed of making a collected edition of his works. He died in 1616, probably of drink taken. Legal documents prove him to have been a lender of small sums, an avid creditor, a would-be encloser of commons. In his will he does not bequeath or mention any books, manuscripts, copyrights, and so forth. It is utterly incredible, then, that this man wrote the poems and plays, so rich in poetry, thought, scholarship, and knowledge, which are attributed to "William Shakespeare." These must be the works of "a concealed poet," a philosopher, a courtier moving in the highest circles, a supreme legist, and, necessarily, a great poet, and student of the classics.

No known person of the age but one, Bacon, was a genius, a legist, a scholar, a great poet, and brilliant courtier, with all the other qualifications so the author of the plays either was Francis Bacon—or some person unknown, who was in all respects equally distinguished, but kept his light under a bushel. Consequently the name "William Shakespeare" is a pseudonym or "pen-name" wisely adopted by Bacon (or the other man) as early as 1593, at a time when William Shakspere was notoriously an actor in the company which produced the plays of the genius styling himself "William Shakespeare."

Let me repeat that, to the best of my powers of understanding and of expression, and in my own words, so as to misquote nobody, I have now summarised the views of the Baconians sans phrase, and of the more cautious or more credulous "Anti-Willians," as I may style the party who deny to Will the actor any share in the authorship of the plays, but do not overtly assign it to Francis Bacon.

Beyond all comparison the best work on the Anti-Willian side of the controversy is The Shakespeare Problem Restated, by Mr. G. G. Greenwood (see my Introduction). To this volume I turn for the exposition of the theory that "Will Shakspere" (with many other spellings) is an actor from the country—a man of very scanty education, in all probability, and wholly destitute of books; while "William Shakespeare," or with the hyphen, "Shake-speare," is a "nom de plume" adopted by the Great Unknown "concealed poet."

When I use the word "author" here, I understand Mr. Greenwood to mean that in the plays called "Shakespearean" there exists work from many pens: owing to the curious literary manners, methods, and ethics of dramatic writing in, say, 1589–1611. In my own poor opinion this is certainly true of several plays in the first collected edition, "The Folio," produced seven years after Will's death, namely in 1623. These curious "collective" methods of play-writing are to be considered later.

Matters become much more perplexing when we examine the theory that "William Shake-speare" (with or without the hyphen), on the title-pages of plays, or when signed to the dedications of poems, is the chosen pen-name, or "nom de plume," of Bacon or of the Unknown.

Here I must endeavour to summarise what Mr. Greenwood has written[14] on the name of the actor, and the "nom de plume" of the unknown author who, by the theory, was not the actor. Let me first confess my firm belief that there is no cause for all the copious writing about the spellings "Shakespeare" or "Shake-speare"—as indicating the true but "concealed poet"—and "Shakspere" (&c.), as indicating the Warwickshire rustic. At Stratford and in Warwickshire the clan-name was spelled in scores of ways, was spelled in different ways within a single document. If the actor himself uniformly wrote "Shakspere" (it seems that we have but five signatures), he was accustomed to seeing the name spelled variously in documents concerning him and his affairs. In London the printers aimed at a kind of uniformity, "Shakespeare" or "Shake-speare": and even if he wrote his own name otherwise, to him it was indifferent. Lawyers and printers might choose their own mode of spelling—and there is no more in the matter.

I must now summarise briefly, in my own words, save where quotations are indicated in the usual way, the results of Mr. Greenwood's researches. "The family of William Shakspere of Stratford" (perhaps it were safer to say "the members of his name") "wrote their name in many different ways—some sixty, I believe, have been noted ... but the form 'Shakespeare' seems never to have been employed by them"; and, according to Mr. Spedding, "Shakspere of Stratford never so wrote his name 'in any known case.'" (According to many Baconians he never wrote his name in his life.) On the other hand, the dedications of Venus and Adonis

---

[14] The Shakespeare Problem Restated, pp. 31–37.

(1593) and of Lucrece (1594) are inscribed "William Shakespeare" (without the hyphen). In 1598, the title-page of Love's Labour's Lost "bore the name W. Shakespere," while in the same year Richard II and Richard III bear "William Shake-speare," with the hyphen (not without it, as in the two dedications by the Author). "The name which appears in the body of the conveyance and of the mortgage bearing" (the actor's) "signature is 'Shakespeare,' while 'Shackspeare' appears in the will, prepared, as we must presume, by or under the directions of Francis Collyns, the Stratford solicitor, who was one of the witnesses thereto" (and received a legacy of £13, 6s. 8d.).

Thus, at Stratford even, the name was spelled, in legal papers, as it is spelled in the two dedications, and in most of the title-pages—and also is spelled otherwise, as "Shackspeare." In March 1594 the actor's name is spelled "Shakespeare" in Treasury accounts. The legal and the literary and Treasury spellings (and conveyances and mortgages and wills are not literature) are Shakespeare, Shackspeare, Shake-speare, Shakespere—all four are used, but we must regard the actor as never signing "Shakespeare" in any of these varieties of spelling—if sign he ever did; at all events he is not known to have used the a in the last syllable.

I now give the essence of Mr. Greenwood's words[15] concerning the nom de plume of the "concealed poet," whoever he was.

"And now a word upon the name 'Shakespeare.' That in this form, and more especially with a hyphen, Shake-speare, the word makes an excellent nom de plume is obvious. As old Thomas Fuller remarks, the name suggests Martial in its warlike sound, 'Hasti-vibrans or Shake-speare.' It is of course further suggestive of Pallas Minerva, the goddess of Wisdom, for Pallas also was a spear-shaker (Pallas ἀπὸ του πάλλειν τὸ δόρυ); and all will remember Ben Jonson's verses... " on Shakespeare's "true-filed lines"—

"In each of which he seems to shake a lance,
As brandished at the eyes of ignorance."

There is more about Pallas in book-titles (to which additions can easily be made), and about "Jonson's Cri-spinus or Cri-spinas," but perhaps we have now the gist of Mr. Greenwood's remarks on the "excellent nom de plume" (cf. pp. 31–37. On the whole of this, cf. The Shakespeare Problem Restated, pp. 293–295; a nom de plume called a "pseudonym," pp. 307, 312; Shakespeare "a mask name," p. 328; a "pseudonym," p. 330; "nom de plume," p. 335).

---

[15] The Shakespeare Problem Restated, pp. 36–37.

Now why was the "nom de plume" or "pseudonym" "William Shakespeare" "an excellent nom de plume" for a concealed author, courtier, lawyer, scholar, and so forth? If "Shakespeare" suggested Pallas Athene, goddess of wisdom and of many other things, and so was appropriate, why add "William"?

In 1593, when the "pseudonym" first appears in Venus and Adonis, a country actor whose name, in legal documents—presumably drawn up by or for his friend, Francis Collyns at Stratford—is written "William Shakespeare," was before the town as an actor in the leading company, that of the Lord Chamberlain. This company produced the plays some of which, by 1598, bear "W. Shakespere," or "William Shakespeare" on their title-pages. Thus, even if the actor habitually spelled his name "Shakspere," "William Shakespeare" was, practically (on the Baconian theory), not only a pseudonym of one man, a poet, but also the real name of another man, a well-known actor, who was not the "concealed poet."

"William Shakespeare" or "Shakespere" was thus, in my view, the ideally worst pseudonym which a poet who wished to be "concealed" could possibly have had the fatuity to select. His plays and poems would be, as they were, universally attributed to the actor, who is represented as a person conspicuously incapable of writing them. With Mr. Greenwood's arguments against the certainty of this attribution I deal later.

Had the actor been a man of rare wit, and of good education and wide reading, the choice of name might have been judicious. A "concealed poet" of high social standing, with a strange fancy for rewriting the plays of contemporary playwrights, might obtain the manuscript copies from their owners, the Lord Chamberlain's Company, through that knowledgeable, witty, and venal member of the company, Will Shakspere. He might then rewrite and improve them, more or less, as it was his whim to do. The actor might make fair copies in his own hand, give them to his company, and say that the improved works were from his own pen and genius. The lie might pass, but only if the actor, in his life and witty talk, seemed very capable of doing what he pretended to have done. But if the actor, according to some Baconians, could not write even his own name, he was impossible as a mask for the poet. He was also impossible, I think, if he were what Mr. Greenwood describes him to be.

Mr. Greenwood, in his view of the actor as he was when he came to London, does not deny to him the gift of being able to sign his name. But, if he were educated at Stratford Free School (of which there is no documentary record), according to Mr. Halliwell-Phillipps "he was removed from school long before the usual age," "in all probability" when "he was about thirteen" (an age at which some boys, later well known, went up to their universities). If we send him to school at seven or so, "it appears that he could only have enjoyed such advantages as it may be supposed to have provided for a period of five or six years at the outside. He was then withdrawn, and, as it seems, put to calf-slaughtering."[16]

What the advantages may have been we try to estimate later.

Mr. Greenwood, with Mr. Halliwell-Phillipps, thinks that Will "could have learned but little there. No doubt boys at Elizabethan grammar schools, if they remained long enough, had a good deal of Latin driven into them. Latin, indeed, was the one subject that was taught; and an industrious boy who had gone through the course and attained to the higher classes would generally be able to write fair Latin prose. But he would learn very little else" (except to write fair Latin prose?). "What we now call 'culture' certainly did not enter into the 'curriculum,' nor 'English,' nor modern languages, nor 'literature.'"[17] Mr. Halliwell-Phillipps says that "removed prematurely from school, residing with illiterate relatives in a bookless neighbourhood, thrown into the midst of occupations adverse to scholastic progress—it is difficult to believe that when he first left Stratford he was not all but destitute of polished accomplishments."[18] Mr. Greenwood adds the apprenticeship to a butcher or draper, but doubts the poaching, and the frequent whippings and imprisonments, as in the story told by the Rev. R. Davies in 1708.[19]

That this promising young man, "when he came to London, spoke the Warwickshire dialect or patois is, then, as certain as anything can be that is incapable of mathematical proof."[20] "Here is the young Warwickshire provincial ... "[21] producing, apparently five or six years after his arrival in town, Venus and Adonis ... "Is it conceivable that this was the work of the Stratford Player of whom we know so little, but of whom we know so much too much? If so we have here a veritable sixteenth-century miracle."[22] Moreover, "our great supposed poet and dramatist had at his death neither book nor manuscript in his possession, or to which he was legally entitled, or in which he had any interest whatever."[23]

---

[16] Tue Shakespeare Problem Restated, p. 20.
[17] The Shakespeare Problem Restated, pp. 47–48.
[18] Ibid., pp. 54–55.
[19] Ibid., p. 54.
[20] Ibid., p. 56.
[21] Ibid., p. 59.
[22] Ibid., p. 62.
[23] Ibid., p. 193.

If it be not conceivable now that the rustic speaking in a patois could write Venus and Adonis, manifestly it was inconceivable in 1593, when Venus and Adonis was signed "William Shakespeare." No man who knew the actor (as described) could believe that he was the author, but there does not exist the most shadowy hint proving that the faintest doubt was thrown on the actor's authorship; ignorant as he was, bookless, and rude of speech. For such a Will as Mr. Greenwood describes to persuade the literary and dramatic world of his age that he did write the plays, would have been a miracle. Consequently Mr. Greenwood has to try to persuade us that there is no sufficient evidence that Will did persuade, say Ben Jonson, of his authorship and we shall see whether or not he works this twentieth-century miracle of persuasion.

Of course if Will were unable to write even his name, as an enthusiastic Baconian asserts, Mr. Greenwood sees that Will could not easily pass for the Author.[24] But his own bookless actor with a patois seems to him, as author of Venus and Adonis, almost inconceivable. Yet, despite Will's bookless rusticity, this poem with Lucrece, which displays knowledge of a work of Ovid not translated into English by 1593, was regarded as his own. I must suppose, therefore, that Will was not manifestly so ignorant of Latin as Mr. Greenwood thinks. "I think it highly probable," says this critic, "that he attended the Grammar School at Stratford" (where nothing but Latin was taught) "for four or five years, and that, later in life, after some years in London, he was probably able to 'bumbast out a line,' and perhaps to pose as 'Poet-Ape that would be thought our chief.' Nay, I am not at all sure that he would not have been capable of collaborating with such a man as George Wilkins, and perhaps of writing quite as well as he, if not even better. But it does not follow from this that he was the author either of Venus and Adonis or of Hamlet."[25]

Nothing follows from all this: we merely see that, in Mr. Greenwood's private opinion, the actor might write even better than George Wilkins, but could not write Venus and Adonis. Will, therefore, though bookless, is not debarred here from the pursuits of literature, in partnership with Wilkins. We have merely the critic's opinion that Will could not write Hamlet, even if, like Wordsworth, "he had the mind," even if the gods had made him more poetical than Wilkins.

Again, "he had had but little schooling; he had 'small Latin and less Greek'" (as Ben Jonson truly says), "but he was a good

---

[24] See his Vindicators of Shakespeare, p. 210.
[25] Vindicators, p. 187.

Johannes Factotum; he could arrange a scene, and, when necessary, 'bumbast out a blank verse.'"[26]

The "Johannes Factotum," who could "bumbast out a blank verse," is taken from Robert Greene's hackneyed attack on an actor-poet, "Shake-scene," published in 1592. "Poet-Ape that would be thought our chief," is from an epigram on an actor-poet by Ben Jonson (1601–16?). If the allusions by Greene and Jonson are to our Will, he, by 1592, had a literary ambition so towering that he thought his own work in the new art of dramatic blank verse was equal to that of Marlowe (not to speak of Wilkins), and Greene reckoned him a dangerous rival to three of his playwright friends, of whom Marlowe is one, apparently.

If Jonson's "Poet-Ape" be meant for Will, by 1601 Will would fain "be thought the chief" of contemporary dramatists. His vanity soared far above George Wilkins! Greene's phrases and Jonson's are dictated by spite, jealousy, and envy; and from them a true view of the work of the man whom they envy, the actor-poet, cannot be obtained. We might as well judge Molière in the spirit of the author of Elomire Hypocondre, and of de Visé! The Anti-Willian arguments keep on appearing, going behind the scenes, and reappearing, like a stage army. To avoid this phenomenon I reserve what is to be said about "Shake-scene" and "Poet-Ape" for another place (pp. 138–145 infra). But I must give the reader a warning. Concerning "William Shakespeare" as a "nom de plume," or pseudonym, Mr. Greenwood says, "Some, indeed, would see through it, and roundly accuse the player of putting forth the works of others as his own. To such he would be a 'Poet-Ape,' or 'an upstart crow' (Shake-scene) 'beautified with the feathers of other writers.'"[27]

If this be true, if "some would see through" (Mr. Greenwood, apparently, means did "see through") the "nom de plume," the case of the Anti-Willians is promising. But, in this matter, Mr. Greenwood se trompe. Neither Greene nor Jonson accused "Shake-scene" or "Poet-Ape" of "putting forth the works of others as his own." That is quite certain, as far as the scorns of Jonson and Greene have reached us. (See pp. 141–145 infra.)

If an actor, obviously incapable of wit and poetry, were credited with the plays, the keenest curiosity would arise in "the profession," and among rival playwrights who envied the wealth and "glory" of the actors. This curiosity, prompting the wits and players to watch and "shadow" Will, would, to put it mildly, most seriously imperil the secret of the concealed author who had the folly to sign

---

[26] The Shakespeare Problem Restated, p. 223.
[27] In Re Shakespeare, p. 54.

himself "William Shakespeare." Human nature could not rest under such a provocation as the "concealed poet" offered.

This is so obvious that had one desired to prove Bacon or the Unknown to be the concealed author, one must have credited his mask, Will, with abundance of wit and fancy, and, as for learning— with about as much as he probably possessed. But the Baconians make him an illiterate yokel, and we have quoted Mr. Greenwood's estimate of the young Warwickshire provincial.

We all have our personal equations in the way of belief. That the plot of the "nom de plume" should have evaded discovery for a week, if the actor were the untutored countryman of the hypotheses, is to me, for one, absolutely incredible. A "concealed poet" looking about for a "nom de plume" and a mask behind which he could be hidden, would not have selected the name, or the nearest possible approach to the name, of an ignorant unread actor. As he was never suspected of not being the author of the plays and poems, Will cannot have been a country ignoramus, manifestly incapable of poetry, wit, and such learning as the plays exhibit. Every one must judge for himself. Mr. Greenwood fervently believes in what I disbelieve.[28]

"Very few Englishmen ... in Elizabethan times, concerned

---

[28] In a brief note of two pages (Cornhill Magazine, November 1911) he makes such reply as the space permits to a paper of my own, "Shakespeare or X?" in the September number. With my goodwill he might have written thirty-two pages to my sixteen, but I am not the Editor, and never heard of Mr. Greenwood's note till May 1912.

He says that I had represented him as stating that the Unknown genius adopted the name of William Shake-speare or Shakespeare "as a good nom de guerre, without any reference to the fact that there was an actor in existence of the name of William Shakspere, whose name was sometimes written Shakespeare, and without the least idea that the works he published under this pseudonym would be fathered upon the actor . . . " (My meaning has obviously been too obscurely stated by me.)

Mr. Greenwood next writes that the confusion between the actor, and the unknown taking the name William Shakespeare, "did happen and was intended to happen."

C'est là le miracle!

How could it happen if the actor were the bookless, ignorant man whom Mr. Greenwood describes? It could not happen: Will must have been unmasked in a day. The fact that a strange plot existed was only too obvious. The Unknown's secret must have been tracked by the hounds of keenest nose in the packs of rival and jealous authors and of actors. None gives tongue.

themselves at all, or cared one brass farthing, about the authorship of plays..." says Mr. Greenwood.

Very few care now. They know the actors' names: in vain, as a rule, do I ask playgoers for the name of the author of their entertainment. But in Elizabeth's time the few who cared were apt to care very much, and they would inquire intensely when the Stratford actor, a bookless, untaught man, was announced as the author of plays which were among the most popular of their day. The seekers never found any other author. They left no hint that they suspected the existence of any other author. Hence I venture to infer that Will seemed to them no unread rustic, but a fellow of infinite fancy,—no scholar to be sure, but very capable of writing the pieces which he fathered.

They may all have been mistaken. Nobody can prove that Heywood and Ben Jonson, and the actors of the Company, were not mistaken. But certain it is that they thought the Will whom they knew capable of the works which were attributed to him. Therefore he cannot possibly have been the man who could not write, of the more impulsive Baconians; or the bookless, and probably all but Latinless, man of Mr. Greenwood's theory. The positions already seem to me to be untenable.

II

THE "SILENCE" ABOUT SHAKESPEARE

Before proceeding further to examine Mr. Greenwood's book, and the Baconian theories, with the careful attention which they deserve, we must clear the ground by explaining two points which appear to puzzle Baconians, though, to be sure, they have their own solutions of the problems.

The first question is: Why, considering that Shakespeare, by the consent of the learned of most of the polite foreign nations, was one of the world's very greatest poets, have we received so few and such brief notices of him from the pens of his contemporaries?

"It is wonderful," exclaims Mr. Crouch-Batchelor, "that hundreds of persons should not have left records of him.[29] We know nearly as much about the most insignificant writer of the period as we know of him, but fifty times more about most of his contemporaries. It is senseless to try to account for this otherwise than by recognising that the man was not the author."

Mr. Crouch-Batchelor is too innocent. He sees the sixteenth century in the colours of the twentieth. We know nothing, except a few dates of birth, death, entrance at school, College, the Inns of Court, and so forth, concerning several of Shakespeare's illustrious contemporaries and successors in the art of dramatic poetry. The Baconians do not quite understand, or, at least, keep steadily before their minds, one immense difference between the Elizabethan age and later times. In 1590–1630, there was no public excitement about the characters, personalities, and anecdotage of merely literary men, poets, and playwrights, who held no position in public affairs, as Spenser did; or in Court, Society, and War, as Sidney did; who did not write about their own feuds and friendships, like Greene and Nash; who did not expand into prefaces and reminiscences, and satires, like Ben Jonson; who never killed anybody, as Ben did; nor were killed, like Marlowe; nor were involved, like him, in charges of atheism, and so forth; nor imprisoned with every chance of having their ears and noses slit, like Marston. Consequently, silence and night obscure the lives and personalities of Kyd, Chapman, Beaumont, Fletcher, Dekker, Webster, and several others, as night and silence hide Shakespeare from our view.

---

[29] Francis Bacon Wrote Shakespeare, p. 37.

He was popular on the stage; some of his plays were circulated separately in cheap and very perishable quartos. No collected edition of his plays appeared during his life; without that he could not be studied, and recognised in his greatness. He withdrew to the country and died. There was no enthusiastic curiosity about him; nobody Boswellised any playwright of his time. The Folio of 1623 gave the first opportunity of studying him as alone he can be studied. The Civil Wars and the Reign of the Saints distracted men's minds and depressed or destroyed the Stage.

Sir William Davenant, a boy when Shakespeare died, used to see the actor at his father's inn at Oxford, was interested in him, and cherished the embers of the drama, which were fading before the theatres were closed. Davenant collected what he could in the way of information from old people of the stage; he told Shakespearean anecdotes in conversation; a few reached the late day when uncritical inquiries began, say 1680–90 at earliest. The memories of ancient people of the theatre and clerks and sextons at Stratford were ransacked, to very little purpose.

As these things were so, how can we expect biographical materials about Shakespeare? As to the man, as to how his character impressed contemporaries, we have but the current epithets: "friendly," "gentle," and "sweet," the praise of his worth by two of the actors in his company (published in 1623), and the brief prose note of Ben Jonson,—this is more than we have for the then so widely admired Beaumont, Ben Jonson's friend, or Chapman, or the adored Fletcher. "Into the dark go one and all," Shakespeare and the others. To be puzzled by and found theories on the silence about Shakespeare is to show an innocence very odd in learned disputants.

The Baconians, as usual, make a puzzle and a mystery out of their own misappreciation of the literary and social conditions of Shakespeare's time. That world could not possibly appreciate his works as we do; the world, till 1623, possessed only a portion of his plays in cheap pamphlets, in several of these his text was mangled and in places unintelligible. And in not a single instance were anecdotes and biographical traits of playwrights recorded, except when the men published matter about themselves, or when they became notorious in some way unconnected with their literary works. Drummond, in Scotland, made brief notes of Ben Jonson's talk; Shakespeare he never met.

That age was not widely and enthusiastically appreciative of literary merit in playwrights who were merely dramatists, and in no other way notorious or eminent. Mr. Greenwood justly says "the contemporary eulogies of the poet afford proof that there were some cultured critics of that day of sufficient taste and acumen to recognise, or partly recognise, his excellence ... "[30] (Here I omit some words, presently to be restored to the text.) From such critics the poet received such applause as has reached us. We also know that the plays were popular; p. 31but the audiences have not rushed to pen and ink to record their satisfaction. With them, as with all audiences, the actors and the spectacle, much more than the "cackle," were the attractions. When Dr. Ingleby says that "the bard of our admiration was unknown to the men of that age," he uses hyperbole, and means, I presume, that he was unknown, as all authors are, to the great majority; and that those who knew him in part made no modern fuss about him.[31]

The second puzzle is,—Why did Shakespeare, conscious of his great powers, never secure for his collected plays the permanence of print and publication? We cannot be sure that he and his company, in fact, did not provide publishers with the copy for the better Quartos or pamphlets of separate plays, as Mr. Pollard argues on good grounds that they sometimes did.[32] For the rest, no dramatic author edited a complete edition of his works before Ben Jonson, a scholarly man, set the example in the year of Shakespeare's, and of Beaumont's death (1616). Neither Beaumont nor Fletcher collected and published their works for the Stage. The idea was unheard of before Jonson set the example, and much of his work lay unprinted till years p. 32after his death. We must remember the conditions of play-writing in Shakespeare's time.

There were then many poets of no mean merit, all capable of admirable verse on occasion; and in various degrees possessed of the lofty, vigorous, and vivid style of that great age. The theatre, and writing for the theatre, afforded to many men of talent a means of livelihood analogous to that offered by journalism among ourselves. They were apt to work collectively, several hands hurrying out a single play; and in twos or threes, or fours or fives, they often collaborated.

As a general rule a play when finished was sold by the author or authors to a company of players, or to a speculator like the notorious Philip Henslowe, and the new owners, "the grand

---

[30] The Shakespeare Problem Restated, p. 333.
[31] In the passage which I quoted, with notes of omission, from Mr. Greenwood (p. 333), he went on to say that the eulogies of the poet by "some cultured critics of that day," "afford no proof that the author who published under the name of Shakespeare was in reality Shakspere the Stratford player." That position I later contest.
[32] See chap. XI, The First Folio.

possessors," were usually averse to the publication of the work, lest other companies might act it. The plays were primarily written to be acted. The company in possession could have the play altered as they pleased by a literary man in their employment.

To follow Mr. Greenwood's summary of the situation "it would seem that an author could restrain any person from publishing his manuscript, or could bring an action against him for so doing, so long as he had not disposed of his right to it; and that the publisher could prevent any other publisher from issuing the work. At the same time it is clear that the law was p. 33frequently violated ... whether because of the difficulty of enforcing it, or through the supineness of authors; and that in consequence authors were frequently defrauded by surreptitious copies of their works being issued by piratical publishers."[33]

It may appear that to "authors" we should, in the case of plays, add "owners," such as theatrical companies, for no case is cited in which such a company brings an action against the publisher of a play which they own. The two players of Shakespeare's company who sign the preface to the first edition of his collected plays (1623, "The First Folio") complain that "divers stolen and surreptitious copies" of single plays have been put forth, "maimed and deformed by the frauds and stealths of injurious impostors." They speak as if they were unable to prevent, or had not the energy to prevent, these frauds. In the accounts of the aforesaid Henslowe, we find him paying forty shillings to a printer to stop or "stay" the printing of a play, Patient Grizel, by three of his hacks.

We perhaps come across an effort of the company to prevent or delay the publication of The Merchant of Venice, on July 17, 1598, in the Stationers' Register. James Robertes, and all other printers, are forbidden to print the book without previous permission from the Lord Chamberlain, the protector of Will Shakespeare's company. Two years passed before Robertes issued p. 34the book.[34] As is well known, Heywood, a most prolific playwright, boasts that he never made a double sale of his pieces to the players and the press. Others occasionally did, which Heywood clearly thought less than honest.

As an author who was also an actor, and a shareholder in his company, Will's interests were the same as theirs. It is therefore curious that some of his pieces were early printed, in quartos, from very good copies; while others appeared in very bad copies, clearly surreptitious. Probably the company gave a good MS. copy,

---

[33] The Shakespeare Problem Restated, pp. 305, 306.
[34] Furness, Merchant of Venice, pp. 271, 272.

sometimes, to a printer who offered satisfactory terms, after the gloss of novelty was off the acted play.[35] In any case, we see that the custom and interests of the owners of manuscript plays ran contrary to their early publication. In 1619 even Ben Jonson, who loved publication, told Drummond that half of his comedies were still unprinted.

These times were not as our own, and must not be judged by ours. Whoever wrote the plays, the actor, or Bacon, or the Man in the Moon; whoever legally owned the manuscripts, was equally incurious and negligent about the preservation of a correct text. As we shall see later, while Baconians urge without any evidence that Bacon himself edited, or gave to Ben Jonson p. 35the duty of editing, the first collected edition (1623), the work has been done in an indescribably negligent and reckless manner, and, as Mr. Greenwood repeatedly states, the edition, in his opinion, contains at least two plays not by his "Shakespeare"—that "concealed poet"—and masses of "non-Shakespearean" work.

How this could happen, if Bacon (as on one hypothesis) either revised the plays himself, or entrusted the task to so strict an Editor as Ben Jonson, I cannot imagine. This is also one of the difficulties in Mr. Greenwood's theory. Thus we cannot argue, "if the actor were the author, he must have been conscious of his great powers. Therefore the actor cannot have been the author, for the actor wholly neglected to collect his printed and to print his manuscript works."

This argument is equally potent against the authorship of the plays by Bacon. He, too, left the manuscripts unpublished till 1623. "But he could not avow his authorship," cry Baconians, giving various exquisite reasons. Indeed, if Bacon were the author, he might not care to divulge his long association with "a cry of players," and a man like Will of Stratford. But he had no occasion to avow it. He had merely to suggest to the players, through any safe channel, that they should collect and publish the works of their old friend Will Shakspere.

Thus indifferent was the main author of the plays, whether he were actor or statesman; and p. 36the actor, at least, is not to blame for the chaos of the first collected edition, made while he was in his grave, and while Bacon was busy in revising and superintending Latin translations of his works on scientific subjects.

We now understand why there are so few contemporary records of Shakspere the man; and see that the neglect of his texts was extreme, whether or not he were the author. The neglect was

---

[35] On this see Mr. Pollard's Shakespeare Folios and Quartos, pp. 1–9.

characteristic of the playwrights of his own and the next generation. In those days it was no marvel; few cared. Nine years passed before a second edition of the collected plays appeared: thirty-two years went by before a third edition was issued—years of war and tumult, yet they saw the posthumous publication of the collected plays of Beaumont and Fletcher.

There remains one more mystery connected with publication. When the first collected edition of the plays appeared, it purported to contain "All His Comedies, Histories, and Tragedies." According to the postulate of the Baconians it was edited by the Author, or by Jonson acting for him. It contains several plays which, according to many critics, are not the author's. This, if true, is mysterious, and so is the fact that a few plays were published, as by Shakespeare, in the lifetime both of the actor and of Bacon; plays which neither acknowledged for his own, for we hear of no remonstrance from— whoever "William Shakespeare" was. It is impossible p. 37for me to say why there was no remonstrance.

Suppose that Will merely supplied Bacon's plays, under his own name, with a slight difference in spelling, to his company. It was as much his interest, in that case, to protest when Bacon's pen-name was taken in vain, as if he had spelled his own surname with an a in the second syllable.

There is another instance which Mr. Greenwood discusses twice.[36] In 1599 Jaggard published "The Passionate Pilgrim; W. Shakespeare." Out of twenty poems, five only were by W. S. In 1612, Jaggard added two poems by Tom Heywood, retaining W. Shakespeare's name as sole author. "Heywood protested" in print, "and stated that Shakespeare was offended, and," says Mr. Greenwood, "very probably he was so; but as he was, so I conceive, 'a concealed poet,' writing under a nom de plume, he seems to have only made known his annoyance through the medium of Heywood."

If so, Heywood knew who the concealed poet was. Turning to pp. 348, 349, we find Mr. Greenwood repeating the same story, with this addition, that the author of the poems published by Jaggard, "to do himself right, hath since published them in his own name." That is, W. Shakespeare has since published under his own name such pieces of The Passionate Pilgrim as p. 38are his own. "The author, I know," adds Heywood, "was much offended with Mr. Jaggard that (altogether unknown to him) presumed to make so bold with his name."

Why was the author so slack when Jaggard, in 1599, published W. S.'s poems with others not by W. S.?

---

[36] The Shakespeare Problem Restated, pp. 202, 348, 349.

How can anyone explain, by any theory? It was as open to him in 1599 as in 1612 to publish his own pieces under his own name, or pen-name.

"Here we observe," says Mr. Greenwood,[37] "that Heywood does nothing to identify 'the author with the player.'" This is, we shall see, the eternal argument. Why should Heywood, speaking of W. Shakespeare, explain what all the world knew? There was no other W. Shakespeare (with or without the e and a) but one, the actor, in the world of letters of Elizabeth and James. Who the author was Heywood himself has told us, elsewhere: the author was—Will!

But why Shakespeare was so indifferent to the use of his name, or, when he was moved, acted so mildly, it is not for me or anyone to explain. We do not know the nature of the circumstances in detail; we do not know that the poet saw hopes of stopping the sale of the works falsely attributed to him. I do not even feel certain that he had not a finger in some of them. Knowing so little, a more soaring wit than mine p. 39might fly to the explanation that "Shakespeare" was the "nom de plume" of Bacon or his unknown equivalent, and that he preferred to "let sleeping dogs lie," or, as Mr. Greenwood might quote the Latin tag, said ne moveas Camarinam.

---

[37] The Shakespeare Problem Restated, p. 349.

III

THAT IMPOSSIBLE HE—THE SCHOOLING OF SHAKESPEARE

The banner-cry of the Baconians is the word "Impossible!" It is impossible that the actor from Stratford (as they think of him, a bookless, untutored lad, speaking in patois) should have possessed the wide, deep, and accurate scholarship displayed by the author of the plays and poems. It is impossible that at the little Free School of Stratford (if he attended it), he should have gained his wide knowledge of the literatures of Greece and Rome. To these arguments, the orthodox Stratfordian is apt to reply, that he finds in the plays and poems plenty of inaccurate general information on classical subjects, information in which the whole literature of England then abounded. He also finds in the plays some knowledge of certain Latin authors, which cannot be proved to have been translated at the date when Shakespeare drew on them. How much Latin Shakespeare knew, in our opinion, will presently be explained.

But, in reply to the Baconians and the Anti-Willians, we must say that while the author of the plays had some lore which scholars also possessed, he did not use his knowledge like a scholar. We do not see how a scholar could make, as the scansion of his blank verse proves that the author did make, the second syllable of the name of Posthumus, in Cymbeline, long. He must have read a famous line in Horace thus,

"Eheu fugaces Posthoome, Posthoome!"

which could scarce 'scape whipping, even at Stratford Free School. In the same way he makes the penultimate syllable of Andronicus short, equally impossible.

Mr. Greenwood, we shall see, denies to him Titus Andronicus, but also appears to credit it to him, as one of the older plays which he "revised, improved, and dressed,"[38] and that is taken to have been all his "authorship" in several cases. A scholar would have corrected, not accepted, false quantities. In other cases, as when Greeks and Trojans cite Plato and Aristotle in Troilus and Cressida, while Plato and Aristotle lived more than a thousand years after the latest conceivable date of the siege of Troy, I cannot possibly suppose that a scholar would have permitted to himself the freak,

---

[38] The Shakespeare Problem Restated, p. 356.

any more than that in The Winter's Tale he should have borrowed from an earlier novel the absurdity of calling Delphi "Delphos" (a non-existent word), of confusing "Delphos" with Delos, and placing the Delphian Oracle in an island. In the same play the author, quite needlessly, makes the artist Giulio Romano (1492–1546) contemporary with the flourishing age of the oracle of the Pythian Apollo. This, at least, would not be ignorance.

We have, I think, sufficient testimony to Ben's inability to refrain from gibes at Shakspere's want of scholarship. Rowe, who had traditions of Davenant's, tells how, in conversation with Suckling, Davenant, Endymion Porter, and Hales of Eton, Ben harped on Will's want of learning; and how Hales snubbed him. Indeed, Ben could have made mirth enough out of The Winter's Tale. For, granting to Mr. Greenwood[39] that "the mention of Delphos suggests the Bohemia of a much earlier date, and under the reign of Ottocar (1255–78) Bohemia extended from the Adriatic to the shores of the Baltic," that only makes matters far worse. "Delphos" never was a place-name; there was no oracle on the isle of "Delphos"; there were no Oracles in 1255–78 (A.D.); and Perdita, who could have sat for her portrait to Giulio Romano, was contemporary with an Oracle at Delphos, but not with Ottocar.

There never was so mad a mixture, not even in Ivanhoe; not even in Kenilworth. Scott erred deliberately, as he says in his prefaces; but Will took the insular oracle of Delphos from Greene, inserted Giulio Romano "for his personal diversion," never heard of Ottocar (no more than I), and made a delightful congeries of errors in gaiety of heart. Nobody shall convince me that Francis Bacon was so charmingly irresponsible; but I cannot speak so confidently of Mr. Greenwood's Great Unknown, a severe scholar, but perhaps a frisky soul. There was no region called Bohemia when the Delphic oracle was in vigour;—this apology (apparently contrived by Sir Edward Sullivan) is the most comic of erudite reflections.

Some cruel critic has censured the lovely speech of Perdita, concerning the flowers which Proserpine let fall, when she was carried off by Dis. How could she, brought up in the hut of a Bohemian shepherd, know anything of the Rape of Proserpine? Why not, as she lived in the days of the Delphic Oracle—and Giulio Romano, and of printed ballads.

It is impossible, Baconians cry, that the rabbit-stealer, brought up among the Audreys and Jaquenettas of Warwickshire, should have created the noble and witty ladies of the Court; and

---

[39] In Re Shakespeare, p. 88, note I.

known the style of his Armado; and understood how dukes and kings talk among themselves—usually in blank verse, it appears.

It is impossible that the home-keeping yokel should have heard of the "obscure" (sic!) Court of Navarre; and known that at Venice there was a place called the Rialto, and a "common ferry" called "the tranect." It is impossible that he should have had "an intimate knowledge of the castle of Elsinore," though an English troupe of actors visited Denmark in 1587. To Will all this knowledge was impossible; for these and many more exquisite reasons the yokel's authorship of the plays is a physical impossibility. But scholars neither invent nor tolerate such strange liberties with time and place, with history, geography, and common sense. Will Shakspere either did not know what was right, or, more probably, did not care, and supposed, like Fielding in the old anecdote, that the audience "would not find it out." How could a scholar do any of these things? He was as incapable of them as Ben Jonson. Such sins no scholar is inclined to; they have, for him, no temptations.

As to Shakspere's schooling, the Baconians point at the current ignorance of Stratford-on-Avon, where many topping burgesses, even aldermen, "made their marks," in place of signing their names to documents. Shakespeare's father, wife, and daughter "made their marks," in place of signing. So did Lady Jane Gordon, daughter of the Earl of Huntly, when she married the cultivated Earl of Bothwell (1566).

There is no evidence, from a roll of schoolboys at Stratford Free Grammar School, about 1564–77, that any given boy attended it; for no roll exists. Consequently there is no evidence that Will was a pupil.

"In the Appendix to Malone's Life of Shakespeare will be found two Latin letters, written by alumni of Stratford School contemporary with Shakespeare," says Mr. Collins.[40] But though the writers were Stratford boys contemporary with Shakespeare, in later life his associates, as there is no roll of pupils' names how do we know, the Baconians may ask, that these men were educated at Stratford School? Why not at Winchester, Eton, St. Paul's, or anywhere? Need one reply?

Mr. Collins goes on, in his simple confiding way, to state that "one letter is by Abraham Sturley, afterwards an alderman of Stratford..." Pursuing the facts, we find that Sturley wrote in Latin to "Richard Quiney, Shakespeare's friend," who, if he could read Sturley's letter, could read Latin. Then young Richard Quiney,

---

[40] Studies in Shakespeare, p. 15; Life of Shakespeare, by Malone, pp. 561–2, 564; Appendix, XI, xvi.

apparently aged eleven, wrote in Latin to his father. If young Richard Quiney be the son of Shakespeare's friend, Richard Quiney, then, of course, his Latin at the age of eleven would only prove that, if he were a schoolboy at Stratford, one Stratford boy could write Latin in the generation following that of Shakespeare. Thus may reason the Baconians.

Perhaps, however, we may say that if Stratford boys contemporary with Shakspere, in his own rank and known to him, learned Latin, which they retained in manhood, Shakspere, if he went to school with them, may have done as much.

Concerning the school, a Free Grammar School, we know that during Shakespeare's boyhood the Mastership was not disdained by Walter Roche, perhaps a Fellow of what was then the most progressive College in learning of those at Oxford, namely, Corpus Christi. That Shakespeare could have been his pupil is uncertain; the dates are rather difficult. I think it probable that he was not, and we do not know the qualifications of the two or three succeeding Masters.

As to the methods of teaching and the books read at Grammar Schools, abundance of information has been collected. We know what the use was in one very good school, Ipswich, from 1528; in another in 1611; but as we do not possess any special information about Stratford School, Mr. Greenwood opposes the admission of evidence from other academies. A man might think that, however much the quality of the teaching varied in various free schools, the nominal curriculum would be fairly uniform.

As to the teacher, a good endowment would be apt to attract a capable man. What was the endowment of Stratford School? It was derived from the bequest of Thomas Jolyffe (died 1482), a bequest of lands in Stratford and Dodwell, and before the Reformation the Brethren of the Guild were "to find a priest fit and able in knowledge to teach grammar freely to all scholars coming to him, taking nothing for their teaching..." "The Founder's liberal endowment made it possible to secure an income for the Master by deed. Under the Reformation, Somerset's Commission found that the School Master had £10 yearly by patent; the school was well conducted, and was not confiscated."[41]

Baconians can compare the yearly £20 (the salary in 1570–6, which then went much further than it does now) with the incomes of other masters of Grammar Schools, and thereby find out if the Head-Master was very cheap. Mr. Elton (who knew his subject

---

[41] C. I. Elton, William Shakespeare, His Family and Friends, pp. 97, 98.

intimately) calls the provision "liberal." The Head-Master of Westminster had £20 and a house.

As to the method of teaching, it was colloquial; questions were asked and answered in Latin. This method, according to Dr. Rouse of Perse School, brings boys on much more rapidly than does our current fashion, as may readily be imagined; but experts vary in opinion. The method, I conceive, should give a pupil a vocabulary. Lilly's Latin Grammar was universally used, and was learned by rote, as by George Borrow, in the last century. See Lavengro for details. Conversation books, Sententiæ Pueriles, were in use; with easy books, such as Corderius's Colloquia, and so on, for boys were taught to speak Latin, the common language of the educated in Europe. Waifs of the Armada, Spaniards wrecked on the Irish coast, met "a savage who knew Latin," and thus could converse with him. The Eclogues of Mantuanus, a Latin poet of the Renaissance (the "Old Mantuan" of Love's Labour's Lost), were used, with Erasmus's Colloquia, and, says Mr. Collins, "such books as Ovid's Metamorphoses" (and other works of his), "the Æneid, selected comedies of Terence and Plautus, and portions of Cæsar, Sallust, Cicero, and Livy."

"Pro-di-gi-ous!" exclaims Mr. Greenwood,[42] referring to what Mr. Collins says Will had read at school. But precocious Latinity was not thought "prodigious" in an age when nothing but Latin was taught to boys—not even cricket. Nor is it to be supposed that every boy read in all of these authors, still less read all of their works, but these were the works of which portions were read. It is not prodigious. I myself, according to my class-master, was "a bad and careless little boy" at thirteen, incurably idle, but I well remember reading in Ovid and Cæsar, and Sallust, while the rest of my time was devoted to the total neglect of the mathematics, English "as she was taught," History, and whatsoever else was expected from me. Shakespeare's time was not thus frittered away; Latin was all he learned (if he went to school), and, as he was (on my theory) a very clever, imaginative kind of boy, I can conceive that he was intensely interested in the stories told by Ovid, and in Catiline's Conspiracy (thrilling, if you know your Sallust); and if his interest were once aroused, he would make rapid progress. My own early hatred of Greek was hissing and malignant, but as soon as I opened Homer, all was changed. One was intensely interested!

Mr. Greenwood will not, in the matter of books, go beyond Mr. Halliwell-Phillipps,[43] "Lilly's Grammar, and a few classical

---

[42] The Shakespeare Problem Restated, p. 44.
[43] The Shakespeare Problem Restated, p. 39.

works chained to the desks of the free schools." Mr. Collins himself gives but "a few classical books," of which portions were read. The chains were in all the free schools, if Mr. Halliwell-Phillipps is right. The chains, if authentic, do not count as objections.

Here it must be noted that Mr. Greenwood's opinion of Will's knowledge and attainments is not easily to be ascertained with precision. He sees, of course, that the pretension of the extreme Baconians—Will could not even write his name—is absurd. If he could not write, he could not pass as the author. Mr. Greenwood "fears that the arguments" (of a most extreme Baconian) "would drive many wandering sheep back to the Stratfordian fold."[44]

He has therefore to find a via media, to present, as the pseudo-author, a Will who possessed neither books nor manuscripts when he made his Testament; a rustic, bookless Will, speaking a patois, who could none the less pass himself off as the author. So "I think it highly probable," says Mr. Greenwood, "that he attended the Grammar School at Stratford for four or five years, and that, later in life, after some years in London, he was probably able to 'bumbast out a line,' and perhaps to pose as 'Poet-Ape who would be thought our chief.'"[45] Again, "He had had but little schooling; he had 'small Latin and less Greek'; but he was a good Johannes Factotum, he could arrange a scene, and, when necessary, 'bumbast out a blank verse.'"[46]

But this is almost to abandon Mr. Greenwood's case. Will appears to me to be now perilously near acceptance as Greene's "Shake-scene," who was a formidable rival to Greene's three professional playwrights: and quite as near to Ben's Poet-Ape "that would be thought our chief," who began by re-making old plays; then won "some little wealth and credit on the scene," who had his "works" printed (for Ben expects them to reach posterity), and whom Ben accused of plagiarism from himself and his contemporaries. But this Shake-scene, this Poet-Ape, is merely our Will Shakespeare as described by bitterly jealous and envious rivals. Where are now the "works" of "Poet-Ape" if they are not the works of Shakespeare which Ben so nobly applauded later, if they are not in the blank verse of Greene's Shake-scene? "Shakespeare's plays" we call them.

When was it "necessary" for the "Stratford rustic" to "bumbast out a blank verse"? Where are the blank verses which he bumbasted out? For what purposes were they bumbasted? By 1592 "Shake-

---

[44] Vindicators of Shakespeare, p. 210.
[45] Vindicators of Shakespeare, p. 187.
[46] Shakespeare Problem Restated, p. 223.

scene" was ambitious, and thought his blank verse as good as the best that Greene's friends, including Marlowe, could write. He had plenty of time to practise before the date when, as Ben wrote, "he would be thought our chief." He would not cease to do that in which he conceived himself to excel; to write for the stage.

When once Mr. Greenwood deems it "highly probable" that Will had four or five years of education at a Latin school, Will has as much of "grounding" in Latin, I think, as would account for all the knowledge of the Roman tongue which he displays. His amount of teaching at school would carry and tempt even a boy who was merely clever, and loved to read romantic tales and comic plays, into Ovid and Plautus—English books being to him not very accessible.

Here I may speak from my own memories, for though utterly idle where set school tasks were concerned, I tried very early to worry the sense out of Aristophanes—because he was said to contain good reading.

To this amount of taste and curiosity, nowise unexampled in an ordinary clever boy, add Genius, and I feel no difficulty as to Will's "learning," such as, at best, it was. "The Stratfordian," says Mr. Greenwood, "will ingeminate 'Genius! Genius!'"[47] I do say "Genius," and stand by it. The ordinary clever boy, in the supposed circumstances, could read and admire his Ovid (though Shakespeare used cribs also), the man of genius could write Venus and Adonis.

Had I to maintain the Baconian hypothesis, I would not weigh heavily on bookless Will's rusticity and patois. Accepting Ben Jonson's account of his "excellent phantasy, brave notions, and gentle expressions, wherein he flowed with that facility ... ," accepting the tradition of his lively wit; admitting that he had some Latin and literature, I would find in him a sufficiently plausible mask for that immense Unknown with a strange taste for furbishing up older plays. I would merely deny to Will his genius, and hand that over to Bacon—or Bungay. Believe me, Mr. Greenwood, this is your easiest way!—perhaps this is your way?—the plot of the unscrupulous Will, and of your astute Bungay, might thus more conceivably escape detection from the pack of envious playwrights.

According to "all tradition," says Mr. Greenwood, Shakespeare was taken from school at the age of thirteen. Those late long-descended traditions of Shakespeare's youth are of little value as evidence; but, if it pleases Mr. Greenwood, I will, for the sake of argument, accept the whole of them. Assuredly I shall not arbitrarily

---

[47] The Shakespeare Problem Restated, p. 69.

choose among the traditions: all depends on the genealogical steps by which they reach us, as far as these can be discovered.[48]

According to the tattle of Aubrey the antiquary, publishing in 1680, an opinion concerning Shakspere's education reached him. It came thus; there had been an actor in Shakspere's company, one Phillips, who, dying in 1605, left to Shakspere the usual thirty-shilling piece of gold; and the same "to my servant, Christopher Beeston." Christopher's son, William, in 1640, became deputy to Davenant in the management of "the King's and Queen's Young Company", and through Beeston, according to Aubrey, Davenant learned; through Beeston Aubrey learned, that Shakespeare "understood Latin pretty well, for he had been in his younger days a school-master in the country." Aubrey writes that "old Mr. Beeston, whom Mr. Dryden calls 'the chronicle of the stage,'" died in 1682.[49]

This is a fair example of the genealogy of the traditions. Phillips, a friend of Shakspere, dies in 1605, leaving a servant, Christopher Beeston (he, too, was a versifier), whose son, William, dies in 1682; he is "the chronicle of the stage." Through him Davenant gets the story, through him Aubrey gets the story, that Shakspere "knew Latin pretty well," and had been a rural dominie. Mr. Greenwood[50] devotes much space to disparaging Aubrey (and I do not think him a scientific authority, moult s'en faut), but Mr. Greenwood here says not a word as to the steps in the descent of the tradition. He frequently repeats himself, thereby forcing me to more iteration than I like. He had already disparaged Aubrey in note I to p. 105, but there he approached so closely to historical method as to say that "Aubrey quotes Beeston, a seventeenth-century actor, as his authority." On p. 209 he dismisses the anecdote (which does not suit his book) as "a mere myth." "He knows, he knows" which traditions are mythical, and which possess a certain historical value.

My own opinion is that Shakspere did "know Latin pretty well," and was no scholar, as his contemporaries reckoned scholarship. He left school, if tradition speak true, by a year later than the age, twelve, when Bacon went to Cambridge. Will, a clever kind of lad (on my theory), left school at an age when some other clever lads became freshmen. Why not? Gilbert Burnet (of whom you may have heard as Bishop of Salisbury under William III) took his degree at the age of fourteen.

Taking Shakspere as an extremely quick, imaginative boy,

---

[48] See chapter X, The Traditional Shakespeare.
[49] See C. I. Elton, William Shakespeare, His Family and Friends, pp. 48, 343–8.
[50] The Shakespeare Problem Restated, pp. 207–9.

with nothing to learn but Latin, and by the readiest road, the colloquial, I conceive him to have discovered that, in Ovid especially, were to be found the most wonderful and delightful stories, and poetry which could not but please his "green unknowing youth." In the years before he left Stratford, and after he left school (1577–87?), I can easily suppose that he was not always butchering calves, poaching, and making love; and that, if he could get books in no other way, this graceless fellow might be detected on a summer evening, knitting his brows over the stories and jests of the chained Ovid and Plautus on his old schoolroom desk. Moi qui parle, I am no genius; but stories, romance, and humour would certainly have dragged me back to the old desks—if better might not be, and why not Shakspere? Put yourself in his place, if you have ever been a lad, and if, as a lad, you liked to steal away into the world of romance, into fairyland.

If Will wrote the plays, he (and indeed whoever wrote the plays) was a marvel of genius. But I am not here claiming for him genius, but merely stating my opinion that if he were fond of stories and romance, had no English books of poetry and romance, and had acquired as much power of reading Latin as a lively, curious boy could easily gain in four years of exclusively Latin education, he might continue his studies as he pleased, yet be, so far, no prodigy.

I am contemplating Will in the conditions on which the Baconians insist; if they will indeed let us assume that for a few years he was at a Latin school. I credit the graceless loon with the curiosity, the prompt acquisitiveness, the love of poetry and romance, which the author of the plays must have possessed in youth. "Tradition says nothing of all that," the Baconian answers, and he may now, if he likes, turn to my reply in The Traditional Shakespeare.[51] Meanwhile, how can you expect old clerks and sextons, a century after date, in a place where literature was not of supreme interest, to retain a tradition that Will used to read sometimes (if he did), in circumstances of privacy? As far as I am able to judge, had I been a boy at Stratford school for four years, had been taught nothing but Latin, and had little or no access to English books of poetry and romance, I should have acquired about the same amount of Latin as I suppose Shakspere to have possessed. Yet I could scarcely, like him, have made the second syllable in "Posthumus" long! Sir Walter Scott, however, was guilty of similar false quantities: he and Shakspere were about equally scholarly.

I suppose, then, that Shakspere's "small Latin" (as Jonson called it) enabled him to read in the works of the Roman clerks; to

---

[51] Chapter X, infra.

read sufficient for his uses. As a fact, he made use of English translations, and also of Latin texts. Scholars like Bacon do not use bad translations of easy Latin authors. If Bacon wanted Plutarch, he went to Plutarch in Greek, not to an English translation of a French translation of a Latin translation.

Some works of Shakespeare, the Lucrece, for example, and The Comedy of Errors (if he were not working over an earlier canvas from a more learned hand), and other passages, show knowledge of Latin texts which in his day had not appeared in published translations, or had not been translated at all as far as we know. In my opinion Will had Latin enough to puzzle out the sense of the Latin, never difficult, for himself. He could also "get a construe," when in London, or help in reading, from a more academic acquaintance: or buy a construe at no high ransom from some poor scholar. No contemporary calls him scholarly; the generation of men who were small boys when he died held him for no scholar. The current English literature of his day was saturated with every kind of classical information; its readers, even if Latinless, knew, or might know a world of lore with which the modern man is seldom acquainted. The ignorant Baconian marvels: the classically educated Baconian who is not familiar with Elizabethan literature is amazed. Really there is nothing worthy of their wonder.

Does any contemporary literary allusion to Shakespeare call him "learned"? He is "sweet," "honey-tongued," "mellifluous," and so forth, but I ask for any contemporary who flattered him with the compliment of "learned." What Ben Jonson thought of his learning (but Ben's standard was very high), what Milton and Fuller, boys of eight when he died, thought of his learning, we know. They thought him "Fancy's child" (Milton) and with no claims to scholarship (Fuller), with "small Latin and less Greek" (Jonson). They speak of Shakespeare the author and actor; not yet had any man divided the persons.

Elizabethan and Jacobean scholarly poets were widely read in the classics. They were not usually, however, scholars in the same sense as our modern scholarly poets and men of letters; such as Mr. Swinburne among the dead, and Mr. Mackail and Sir Gilbert Murray—if I may be pardoned for mentioning contemporary names. But Elizabethan scholarly poets, and Milton, never regarded Shakespeare as learned. Perhaps few modern men of letters who are scholars differ from them. The opinion of Mr. Collins is to be discussed presently, but even he thought Shakespeare's scholarship "inexact," as we shall see.

I conceive that Shakspere "knew Latin pretty well," and, on Ben Jonson's evidence, he knew "less Greek." That he knew any

Greek is surprising. Apparently he did, to judge from Ben's words. My attitude must, to the Baconians, seem frivolous, vexatious, and evasive. I cannot pretend to know what was Shakspere's precise amount of proficiency in Latin when he was writing the plays. That between his own knowledge, and construes given to him, he might easily get at the meaning of all the Latin, not yet translated, which he certainly knew, I believe.

Mr. Greenwood says "the amount of reading which the lad Shakspere must have done, and assimilated, during his brief sojourn at the Free School is positively amazing."[52] But I have shown how an imaginative boy, with little or no access to English poetry and romances, might continue to read Latin "for human pleasure" after he left school. As a professional writer, in a London where Latinists were as common as now they are rare in literary society, he might read more, and be helped in his reading. Any clever man might do as much, not to speak of a man of genius. "And yet, alas, there is no record or tradition of all this prodigious industry...." I am not speaking of "prodigious industry," and of that—at school. In a region so non-literary as, by his account, was Stratford, Mr. Greenwood ought not to expect traditions of Will's early reading (even if he studied much more deeply than I have supposed) to exist, from fifty to seventy years after Will was dead, in the memories of the sons and grandsons of country people who cared for none of these things. The thing is not reasonable.[53]

Let me take one example[54] of what Mr. E. A. Sonnenschein is quoted as saying (somewhere) about Shakespeare's debt to Seneca's then untranslated paper De Clementia (1, 3, 3; I, 7, 2; I, 6, I). It inspires Portia's speech about Mercy. Here I give a version of the Latin.

"Clemency becometh, of all men, none more than the King or chief magistrate (principem) ... No one can think of anything more becoming to a ruler than clemency ... which will be confessed the fairer and more goodly in proportion as it is exhibited in the higher office ... But if the placable and just gods punish not instantly with their thunderbolts the sins of the powerful, how much more just it is that a man set over men should gently exercise his power. What? Holds not he the place nearest to the gods, who, bearing himself like the gods, is kind, and generous, and uses his power for the better? ... Think ... what a lone desert and waste Rome would be, were nothing left, and none, save such as a severe judge would absolve."

---

[52] The Shakespeare Problem Restated, p. 96.
[53] See chapter X, The Traditional Shakespeare.
[54] The Shakespeare Problem Restated, pp. 94–96.

The last sentence is fitted with this parallel in Portia's speech:

> "Consider this
> That in the course of Justice none of us
> Should see salvation."

Here, at least, Protestant theology, not Seneca, inspires Portia's eloquence.

Now take Portia:

> "The quality of Mercy is not strain'd;
> It droppeth as the gentle rain from heaven
> Upon the place beneath: it is twice blessed;
> It blesseth him that gives and him that takes;"

(Not much Seneca, so far!)

> "'Tis mightiest in the mightiest; it becomes
> The thronèd monarch better than his crown;
> His sceptre shows the force of temporal power,
> The attribute to awe and majesty,
> Wherein doth sit the dread and fear of kings;
> But Mercy is above this sceptred sway,
> It is enthronèd in the hearts of kings,
> It is an attribute to God himself;
> And earthly power doth then show likest God's,
> When mercy seasons justice..."

There follows the passage about none of us seeing salvation, already cited, and theological in origin.

Whether Shakespeare could or could not have written these reflections, without having read Seneca's De Clementia, whether, if he could not conceive the ideas "out of his own head," he might not hear Seneca's words translated in a sermon, or in conversation, or read them cited in an English book, each reader must decide for himself. Nor do I doubt that Shakespeare could pick out what he wanted from the Latin if he cast his eye over the essay of the tutor of Nero.

My view of Shakespeare's Latinity is much like that of Sir Walter Raleigh.[55] As far as I am aware, it is the opinion usually held by people who approach the subject, and who have had a classical education. An exception was the late Mr. Churton Collins, whose ideas are discussed in the following chapter.

---

[55] Shakespeare, pp. 38–40.

In his youth, and in the country, Will could do what Hogg and Burns did (and Hogg had no education at all; he was self-taught, even in writing). Will could pick up traditional, oral, popular literature. "His plays," says Sir Walter Raleigh, "are extraordinarily rich in the floating debris of popular literature,—scraps and tags and broken ends of songs and ballads and romances and proverbs. In this respect he is notable even among his contemporaries... . Edgar and Iago, Petruchio and Benedick, Sir Toby and Pistol, the Fool in Lear and the Grave-digger in Hamlet, even Ophelia and Desdemona, are all alike singers of old songs... . "[56] He is rich in rural proverbs not recorded in Bacon's Promus.

Shakespeare in the country, like Scott in Liddesdale, "was making himself all the time."

The Baconian will exclaim that Bacon was familiar with many now obsolete rural words. Bacon, too, may have had a memory rich in all the tags of song, ballad, story, and dicton. But so may Shakespeare.

---

[56] Raleigh, Shakespeare, pp. 77, 78.

IV

MR. COLLINS ON SHAKESPEARE'S LEARNING

That Shakspere, whether "scholar" or not, had a very wide and deep knowledge both of Roman literature and, still more, of the whole field of the tragic literature of Athens, is a theory which Mr. Greenwood seems to admire in that "violent Stratfordian," Mr. Churton Collins.[57] I think that Mr. Collins did not persuade classical scholars who have never given a thought to the Baconian belief, but who consider on their merits the questions: Does Shakespeare show wide classical knowledge? Does he use his knowledge as a scholar would use it?

My friend, Mr. Collins, as I may have to say again, was a very wide reader of poetry, with a memory like Macaulay's. It was his native tendency to find coincidences in poetic passages (which, to some, to me for example, did not often seem coincidental); and to explain coincidences by conscious or subconscious borrowing. One remarked in him these tendencies long before he wrote on the classical acquirements of Shakespeare.

While Mr. Collins tended to account for similarities in the work of authors by borrowing, my tendency was to explain them as undesigned coincidences. The question is of the widest range. Some inquirers explain the often minute coincidences in myths, popular tales, proverbs, and riddles, found all over the world, by diffusion from a single centre (usually India). Others, like myself, do not deny cases of transmission, but in other cases see spontaneous and independent, though coincident invention. I do not believe that the Arunta of Central Australia borrowed from Plutarch the central feature of the myth of Isis and Osiris.

It is not on Shakespeare's use, now and then, of Greek and Latin models and sources, but on coincidences detected by Mr. Collins himself, and not earlier remarked, that he bases his belief in the saturation of Shakespeare's mind with Roman and Athenian literature. Consequently we can only do justice to Mr. Collins's system, if we compare example after example of his supposed instances of Shakespeare's borrowing. This is a long and irksome

---

[57] So he seems to me to do; but in Vindicators of Shakespeare, p. 135, he shows great caution: "I refer the reader to Mr. Collin's essay, and ask him to judge for himself."

task; and the only fair plan is for the reader to peruse Mr. Collins's Studies in Shakespeare, compare the Greek and Roman texts, and weigh each example of supposed borrowing for himself. Baconians must delight in this labour.

I shall waive the question whether it were not possible for Shakespeare to obtain a view of the manuscript translation of plays of Plautus made by Warner for his unlearned friends, and so to use the Menæchmi as the model of The Comedy of Errors. He does not borrow phrases from it, as he does from North's Plutarch.

Venus and Adonis owes to Ovid, at most, but ideas for three purple patches, scattered in different parts of the Metamorphoses. Lucrece is based on the then untranslated Fasti of Ovid. I do not think Shakespeare incapable of reading such easy Latin for himself; or too proud to ask help from a friend, or buy it from some poor young University man in London. That is a simple and natural means by which he could help himself when in search of a subject for a play or poem; and ought not to be overlooked.

Mr. Collins, in his rapturous account of Shakespeare's wide and profound knowledge of the classics, opens with the remark: "Nothing which Shakespeare has left us warrants us in pronouncing with certainty that he read the Greek classics in the original, or even that he possessed enough Greek to follow the Latin versions of those classics in the Greek text."[58] In that case, how did Shakespeare's English become contaminated, as Mr. Collins says it did, with Greek idioms, while he only knew the Greek plays through Latin translations?

However this is to be answered, Mr. Collins proceeds to prove Shakespeare's close familiarity with Latin and with Greek dramatic literature by a method of which he knows the perils—"it is always perilous to infer direct imitation from parallel passages which may be mere coincidences."[59] Yet this method is what he practises throughout; with what amount of success every reader must judge for himself.

He thinks it "surely not unlikely" that Polonius's

"Neither a borrower nor a lender be:
For loan oft loses both itself and friend,"

may be a terse reminiscence of seven lines in Plautus (Trinummus, iv. 3). Why, Polonius is a coiner of commonplaces, and if ever there

---

[58] Studies in Shakespeare, p. 15.
[59] Studies in Shakespeare, p. 21.

were a well-known reflection from experience it is this of the borrowers and lenders.

Next, take this of Plautus (Pseudolus, I, iv. 7–10), "But just as the poet when he has taken up his tablets seeks what exists nowhere among men, and yet finds it, and makes that like truth which is mere fiction." We are to take this as the possible germ of Theseus's theory of the origin of the belief in fairies:

> "And as imagination bodies forth
> The forms of things unknown, the poet's pen
> Turns them to shapes, and gives to airy nothing
> A local habitation and a name."

The reasoning is odd; imagination bodies forth forms, and the poet's pen turns them to shapes. But to suppose that Shakespeare here borrowed from Plautus appears highly superfluous.

These are samples of Mr. Collins's methods throughout.

Of Terence there were translations—first in part; later, in 1598, of the whole. Of Seneca there was an English version (1581). Mr. Collins labours to show that one passage "almost certainly" implies Shakespeare's use of the Latin; but it was used "by an inexact scholar,"—a terribly inexact scholar, if he thought that "alienus" ("what belongs to another") meant "slippery"!

Most of the passages are from plays (Titus Andronicus and Henry VI, i., ii., iii.), which Mr. Greenwood denies (usually) to his author, the Great Unknown. Throughout these early plays Mr. Collins takes Shakespeare's to resemble Seneca's Latin style: Shakespeare, then, took up Greek tragedy in later life; after the early period when he dealt with Seneca. Here is a sample of borrowing from Horace, "Persicos odi puer apparatus" (Odes. I, xxxviii. I). Mr. Collins quotes Lear (III, vi. 85) thus, "You will say they are Persian attire." Really, Lear in his wild way says to Edgar, "I do not like the fashion of your garments: you will say they are Persian; but let them be changed." Mr. Collins changes this into "you will say they are Persian attire," a phrase "which could only have occurred to a classical scholar." The phrase is not in Shakespeare, and Lear's wandering mind might as easily select "Persian" as any other absurdity.

So it is throughout. Two great poets write on the fear of death, on the cries of new-born children, on dissolution and recombination in nature, on old age; they have ideas in common, obvious ideas, glorified by poetry,—and Shakespeare, we are told, is borrowing from Lucretius or Juvenal; while the critic leaves his reader to find out and study the Latin passages which he does not quote. So arbitrary is taste in these matters that Mr. Collins, like Mr. Grant White, but independently, finds Shakespeare putting a thought from the Alcibiades I of Plato into the mouth of Achilles in Troilus and Cressida, while Mr. J. M. Robertson suggests that the borrowing is from Seneca—where Mr. Collins does not find "the smallest parallel." Mr. Collins is certainly right; the author of Troilus makes Ulysses quote Plato as "the author" of a remark, and makes Achilles take up the quotation, which Ulysses goes on to criticise.

Thus, in this play, not only Aristotle (as Hector says) but Plato are taken to have lived before the Trojan war, and to have been read by the Achæans!

There were Latin translations of Plato; the Alcibiades I was published apart, from Ficinus' version, in 1560, with the sub-title, Concerning the Nature of Man. Who had read it?—Shakespeare, or one of the two authors (Dekker and Chettle) of another Troilus and Cressida (now lost), or Bacon, or Mr. Greenwood's Unknown? Which of these Platonists chose to say that Plato and Aristotle lived long before Homer? Which of them followed the Ionic and mediæval anti-Achæan view of Homer's heroes, as given in the Troy Books of the Middle Ages, and yet knew Iliad, Book VII, and admired Odysseus, whom the Ionian tradition abhors? Troilus and Cressida is indeed a mystery, but Somebody concerned in it had read Ficinus' version of the Alcibiades;[60] and yet made the monstrous anachronism of dating Aristotle and Plato before the Trojan war. "That was his fun," as Charles Lamb said in another connection.

Mr. Collins, it is plain, goes much further than the "small Latin" with which his age (like myself) credited Shakespeare. He could read Latin, Mr. Collins thinks, as easily as an educated Briton reads French—that is, as easily as he reads English. Still further, Shakespeare, through Latin translations, was so saturated with the Greek drama "that the characteristics which differentiate his work from the work of his contemporaries and recall in essentials the work of the Greek dramatists are actually attributable to these dramatists."

Ben Jonson, and all the more or less well-taught University wits, as far as I remember, like Greene, Marlowe, and Lyly, do not show much acquaintance with Euripides, Æschylus, Sophocles, and do not often remind us of these masters. Shakespeare does remind us of them—the only question is, do the resemblances arise from his possession of a genius akin to that of Greece, or was his memory so

---

[60] Alcibiades, I, pp. 132, 133; Troilus, III, scene 3.

stored with all the treasures of their art that the waters of Helicon kept bubbling up through the wells of Avon?

But does Mr. Collins prove (what, as he admits, cannot be demonstrated) that Shakespeare was familiar with the Attic tragedians? He begins by saying that he will not bottom his case "on the ground of parallels in sentiment and reflection, which, as they express commonplaces, are likely to be" (fortuitous) "coincidences." Three pages of such parallels, all from Sophocles, therefore follow. "Curiously close similarities of expression" are also barred. Four pages of examples therefore follow, from Sophocles and Æschylus, plays and fragments, Euripides, and Homer too (once!). Again, "identities of sentiment under similar circumstances" are not to be cited; two pages are cited; and "similarities, however striking they may be in metaphorical expression," cannot safely be used; several pages of them follow.

Finally, Mr. Collins chooses a single play, the Aias of Sophocles, and tests Shakespeare by that, unluckily in part from Titus Andronicus, which Mr. Greenwood regards (usually) as non-Shakespearean, or not by his unknown great author. Troilus and Cressida, whatever part Shakespeare may have had in it, does suggest to me that the author or authors knew of Homer no more than the few books of the Iliad, first translated by Chapman and published in 1598. But he or they did know the Aias of Sophocles, according to Mr. Collins: so did the author of Romeo and Juliet.

Now all these sorts of parallels between Shakespeare and the Greeks are, Mr. Collins tells us, not to count as proofs that Shakespeare knew the Greek tragedians. "We have obviously to be on our guard"[61] against three kinds of such parallels, which "may be mere coincidences,"[62] fortuitous coincidences. But these coincidences against which "we must be on our guard" fill sixteen pages (pp. 46–63). These pages must necessarily produce a considerable effect in the way of persuading the reader that Shakespeare knew the Greek tragedians as intimately as Mr. Collins did. Mr. Greenwood is obliged to leave these parallels to readers of Mr. Collins's essay. Indeed, what more can we do? Who would read through a criticism of each instance? Two or three may be given. The Queen in Hamlet reminds that prince, grieving for his father's death, that "all that live must die":

> "That loss is common to the race,
> And common is the common-place."

---

[61] Studies in Shakespeare, p. 46.
[62] Iliad, p. 63.

The Greek Chorus offers the commonplace to Electra,—and here is a parallel! Again, two Greeks agree with Shakespeare that anxious expectation of evil is worse than actual experience thereof. Greece agrees with Shakespeare that ill-gotten gains do not thrive, or that it is not lucky to be "a corby messenger" of bad news; or that all goes ill when a man acts against his better nature; or that we suffer most from the harm which we bring on ourselves; or that there is strength in a righteous cause; or that blood calls for blood (an idea common to Semites, Greeks, and English readers of the Bible); or that, having lost a very good man, you will not soon see his like again,—and so on as long as you please. Of such wisdom are proverbs made, and savages and Europeans have many parallel proverbs. Vestigia nulla retrorsum is as well known to Bushmen as to Latinists. Manifestly nothing in this kind proves, or even suggests, that Shakespeare was saturated in Greek tragedy. But page on page of such facts as that both Shakespeare and Sophocles talk, one of "the belly-pinched wolf," the other of "the empty-bellied wolf," are apt to impress the reader—and verily both Shakespeare and Æschylus talk of "the heart dancing for joy." Mr. Collins repeats that such things are no proof, but he keeps on piling them up. It was a theory of Shakespeare's time that the apparent ghost of a dead man might be an impersonation of him by the devil. Hamlet knows this—

"The spirit that I have seen may be the devil."

Orestes (Electra, Euripides) asks whether it may not be an avenging dæmon (alastor) in the shape of a god, that bids him avenge his father. Is Shakespeare borrowing from Euripides, or from a sermon, or any contemporary work on ghosts, such as that of Lavater?

A girl dies or is sacrificed before her marriage, and characters in Romeo and Juliet, and in Euripides, both say that Death is her bridegroom. Anyone might say that, anywhere, as in the Greek Anthology—

"For Death not for Love hast thou loosened thy zone."

One needs the space of a book wherein to consider such parallels. But confessedly, though a parade is made of them, they do not prove that Shakespeare constantly read Greek tragedies in Latin translations.

To let the truth out, the resemblances are mainly found in such commonplaces: as when both Aias and Antony address the Sun of their latest day in life; or when John of Gaunt and Aias both pun on their own names.

The situations, in Hamlet and the Choephoræ and Electra, are so close that resemblances in some passages must and do occur, and Mr. Collins does not comment specially upon the closest resemblance of all: the English case is here the murder of Duncan, the Greek is the murder of Agamemnon.

Now it would be easy for me to bring forward many close parallels between Homer and the old Irish epic story of Cuchulainn, between Homer and Beowulf and the Njal's saga, yet Norsemen and the early Irish were not students of Homer! The parallel passages in Homer, on one side, and the Old Irish Tain Bo Cualgne, and the Anglo-Saxon epics, are so numerous and close that the theory of borrowing from Homer has actually occurred to a distinguished Greek scholar. But no student of Irish and Anglo-Saxon heroic poetry has been found, I think, to suggest that Early Irish and Anglo-Saxon Court minstrels knew Greek. The curious may consult Mr. Munro Chadwick's The Heroic Age (1912), especially Chapter XV, "The Common Characteristics of Teutonic and Greek Heroic Poetry," and to what Mr. Chadwick says much might be added.

But, to be short, Mr. Collins's case can only be judged by readers of his most interesting Studies in Shakespeare. To me, Hamlet's soliloquy on death resembles a fragment from the Phœnix of Euripides no more closely than two sets of reflections by great poets on the text that "of death we know nothing" are bound to do,—though Shakespeare's are infinitely the richer. For Shakespeare's reflections on death, save where Christians die in a Christian spirit, are as agnostic as those of the post-Æschylean Greek and early Anglo-Saxon poets. In many respects, as Mr. Collins proves, Shakespeare's highest and deepest musings are Greek in tone. But of all English poets he who came nearest to Greece in his art was Keats, who of Greek knew nothing. In the same way, a peculiar vein of Anglo-Saxon thought, in relation to Destiny and Death, is purely Homeric, though necessarily unborrowed; nor were a native Fijian poet's lines on old age, sine amore jocisque, borrowed from Mimnermus! There is such a thing as congruity of genius. Mr. Collins states the hypothesis—not his own—"that by a certain natural affinity Shakespeare caught also the accent and tone as well as some of the most striking characteristics of Greek tragedy."

Though far from accepting most of Mr. Collins's long array of Greek parallels, I do hold that by "natural affinity," by congruity of genius, Shakespeare approached and resembled the great Athenians.

One thing seems certain to me. If Shakspere read and borrowed from Greek poetry, he knew it as well (except Homer) as

Mr. Collins knew it; and remembered what he knew with Mr. Collins's extraordinary tenacity of memory.

Now if "Shakespeare" did all that, he was not the actor. The author, on Mr. Collins's showing, must have been a very sedulous and diligent student of Greek poetry, above all of the drama, down to its fragments. The Baconians assuredly ought to try to prove, from Bacon's works, that he was such a student.

Mr. Collins, "a violent Stratfordian," overproved his case. If his proofs be accepted, Shakspere the actor knew the Greek tragedians as well as did Mr. Swinburne. If the author of the plays were so learned, the actor was not the author, in my opinion—he was, in the opinion of Mr. Collins.

If Shakespeare's spirit and those of Sophocles and Æschylus meet, it is because they move on the same heights, and thence survey with "the poet's sad lucidity" the same "pageant of men's miseries." But how dissimilar in expression Shakespeare can be, how luxuriant and apart from the austerity of Greece, we observe in one of Mr. Collins's parallels.

Polynices, in the Phœnissæ of Euripides (504–506), exclaims:

> "To the stars' risings, and the sun's I'd go,
> And dive 'neath earth,—if I could do this thing,—
> Possess Heaven's highest boon of sovereignty."

Then compare Hotspur:

> "By Heaven, methinks it were an easy leap
> To pluck bright honour from the pale faced moon,
> Or dive into the bottom of the deep,
> Where fathom-line could never touch the ground,
> And pluck up drownèd honour by the locks,
> So he that doth redeem her thence, might wear
> Without corrival all her dignities."

What a hurrying crowd of pictures rush through Hotspur's mind! Is Shakespeare thinking of the Phœnissæ, or is he speaking only on the promptings of his genius?

V

SHAKESPEARE, GENIUS, AND SOCIETY

A phrase has been used to explain the Greek element in Shakespeare's work, namely, "congruity of genius," which is apt to be resented by Baconians. Perhaps they have a right to resent it, for "genius" is hard to define, and genius is invoked by some wild wits to explain feats of Shakespeare's which (to Baconians) appear "miracles." A "miracle" also is notoriously hard to define; but we may take it ("under all reserves") to stand for the occurrence of an event, or the performance of an action which, to the speaker who applies the word "miracle," seems "impossible." The speaker therefore says, "The event is impossible; miracles do not happen: therefore the reported event never occurred. The alleged performance, the writing of the plays by the actor, was impossible, was a miracle, therefore was done by some person or persons other than the actor." This idea of the impossibility of the player's authorship is the foundation of the Baconian edifice.

I have, to the best of my ability, tried to describe Mr. Greenwood's view of the young provincial from Warwickshire, Will Shakspere. If Will were what Mr. Greenwood thinks he was, then Will's authorship of the plays seems to me, "humanly speaking," impossible. But then Mr. Greenwood appeared to omit from his calculations the circumstance that Will may have been, not merely "a sharp boy" but a boy of great parts; and not without a love of stories and poetry: a passion which, in a bookless region, could only be gratified through folk-song, folk-tale, and such easy Latin as he might take the trouble to read. If we add to these very unusual but not wholly impossible tastes and abilities, that Will may have been a lad of genius, there is no more "miracle" in his case than in other supreme examples of genius. "But genius cannot work miracles, cannot do what is impossible." Do what is impossible to whom? To the critics, the men of common sense.

Alas, all this way of talking about "miracles," and "the impossible," and "genius" is quite vague and popular. What do we mean by "genius"? The Latin term originally designates, not a man's everyday intellect, but a spirit from without which inspires him, like the "Dæmon," or, in Latin, "Genius" of Socrates, or the lutin which rode the pen of Molière. "Genius" is claimed for Shakespeare in an inscription on his Stratford monument, erected at latest some six years after his death. Following this path of thought we come to "inspiration": the notion of it, as familiar to Australian savages as to any modern minds, is that, to the poet, what he produces is given by some power greater than himself, by the Boilyas (spirits) or Pundjel, the Father of all. This palæolithic psychology, of course, is now quite discredited, yet the term "genius" is still (perhaps superstitiously) applied to the rare persons whose intellectual faculties lightly outrun those of ordinary mortals, and who do marvels with means apparently inadequate.

In recent times some philosophers, like Mr. F. W. H. Myers, put—in place of the Muses or the Boilyas, or the Genius—what they call the "Subliminal Self," something "far more deeply interfused than the everyday intellect." This subconscious self, capable of far more than the conscious intelligence, is genius.

On the other side, genius may fairly be regarded as faculty, only higher in degree, and not at all different in kind, from the everyday intellect which, for example, pens this page.

Thus as soon as we begin to speak of "genius," we are involved in speculations, psychological, psychical, physical, and metaphysical; in difficulties of all sorts not at present to be solved either by physiological science or experimental psychology, or by psychical research, or by the study of heredity. When I speak of "the genius of Shakespeare," of Jeanne d'Arc, of Bacon, even of Wellington, I possibly have a meaning which is not in all respects the meaning of Mr. Greenwood, when he uses the term "genius"; so we are apt to misunderstand each other. Yet we all glibly use the term "genius," without definition and without discussion.

At once, too, in this quest, we jostle against "that fool of a word," as Napoleon said, "impossible." At once, on either side, we assume that we know what is possible and what is impossible,—and so pretend to omniscience.

Thus some "Stratfordians," or defenders of the actor's authorship, profess to know—from all the signed work of Bacon, and from all that has reached us about Bacon's occupations and preoccupations, from 1590 to 1605—that the theory of Bacon's authorship of the plays is "impossible." I, however, do not profess this omniscience.

On the other side the Baconian, arguing from all that he knows, or thinks he knows, or can imagine, of the actor's education, conditions of life, and opportunities, argues that the authorship of the actor is "impossible."

Both sides assume to be omniscient, but we incontestably know much more about Bacon, in his works, his aims, his inclinations, and in his life, than we know about the actor; while about "the potentialities of genius," we know—very little.

Thus, with all Bacon's occupations and preoccupations, he had, the Baconians will allow, genius. By the miracle of genius he may have found time and developed inclination, to begin by furbishing up older plays for a company of actors: he did it extremely well, but what a quaint taste for a courtier and scholar! The eccentricities of genius may account for his choice of a "nom de plume," which, if he desired concealment, was the last that was likely to serve his turn. He may also have divined all the Doll Tearsheets and Mrs. Quicklys and Pistols, whom, conceivably, he did not much frequent.

I am not one of those who deny that Bacon might have written Hamlet "if he had the mind," as Charles Lamb said of Wordsworth. Not at all; I am the last to limit the potentialities of genius.

But suppose, merely for the sake of argument, that Will Shakspere too had genius in that amazing degree which, in Henry V, the Bishop of Ely and the Archbishop of Canterbury describe and discuss in the case of the young king. In this passage we perceive that the poet had brooded over and been puzzled by the "miracle" (he uses the word) of genius. Says Canterbury speaking of the Prince's wild youth,

> "Never was such a sudden scholar made."

One Baconian objection to Shakespeare's authorship is that during his early years in London (say 1587–92) he was "such a sudden scholar made" in various things.

The young king's

> "addiction was to courses vain,
> His companies unletter'd, rude, and shallow,"

precisely like Shakespeare's courses and companions at Stratford

> "Had never noted in him any study."

Stratford tradition, a century after Shakespeare left the town, did not remember "any study" in him; none had been "noted," nor could have been remembered. To return to Henry, he shines in divinity, knowledge of "commonwealth affairs,"

> "You would say, it hath been all in all his study."

He is as intimate with the art of war; to him "Gordian knots of policy" are "familiar as his garter." He must have

> "The art and practic part of life,"

as "mistress to this theorie,"

"Which is a wonder how his Grace should glean it,"

as his youth was riotous, and was lived in all men's gaze,

> "And never noted in him any study,
> Any retirement, any sequestration
> From open haunts and popularity."

The Bishop of Ely can only suggest that Henry's study or "contemplation"

> "Grew like the summer grass, fastest by night,
> Unseen,"

and Canterbury says

> "It must be so, for miracles are ceased."

And thus the miracle of genius baffles the poet, for Henry's had been "noisy nights," notoriously noisy.

Now, as we shall later show, Bacon's rapid production of the plays, considering his other contemporary activities and varied but always absorbing interests, was as much a miracle as the sudden blossoming of Henry's knowledge and accomplishments; for all Bacon's known exertions and occupations, and his deepest and most absorbing interest, were remote from the art of tragedy and comedy. If we are to admit the marvel of genius in Bacon, of whose life and pursuits we know much, by parity of reasoning we may grant that the actor, of whom we know much less, may have had genius: had powers and could use opportunities in a way for which Baconians make no allowance.

We now turn to Mr. Greenwood's chapter, "Shakespeare and 'Genius.'" It opens with the accustomed list of poor Will's disqualifications, "a boy born of illiterate parents," but we need not rehearse the list.[63] He "comes to town" (date unknown) "a needy adventurer"; in 1593 appeared the poem Venus and Adonis, author's name being printed as "W. Shakespeare." Then comes Lucrece (1594). In 1598 Love's Labour's Lost, printed as "corrected and augmented" by "W. Shakespere." And so on with all the rest. Criticism of the learning and splendour of the two poems follows. To Love's Labour's Lost, and the amusing things written about it by Baconians, I return; and to Shakespeare's "impossible" knowledge

---

[63] The Shakespeare Problem Restated, pp. 54, 55.

of courtly society, his "polish and urbanity," his familiar acquaintance with contemporary French politics, foreign proverbs, and "the gossip of the Court" of Elizabeth: these points are made by His Honour Judge Webb.

All this lore to Shakespeare is "impossible"—he could not read, say some Baconians, or had no Latin, or had next to none; on these points I have said my say. The omniscient Baconians know that all the early works ascribed to the actor were impossible, to a man of, say thirty—who was no more, and knew no more, than they know that the actor was and knew; and as for "Genius," it cannot work miracles. Genius "bestows upon no one a knowledge of facts," "Shakespeare, however favoured by nature, could impart only what he had learned."

Precisely, but genius as I understand it (and even cleverness) has a way of acquiring knowledge of facts where the ordinary "dull intelligent man" gains none. Keen interest, keen curiosity, swift observation, even the power of tearing out the things essential from a book, the gift of rapid reading; the faculty of being alive to the fingertips,—these, with a tenacious memory, may enable a small boy to know more facts of many sorts than his elders and betters and all the neighbours. They are puzzled, if they make the discovery of his knowledge. Scott was such a small boy; whether we think him a man of genius or not. Shakspere, even the actor, was, perhaps, a man of genius, and possessed this power of rapid acquisition and vivid retention of all manner of experience and information. To what I suppose to have been his opportunities in London, I shall return. Meanwhile, let the doubter take up any popular English books of Shakespeare's day: he will find them replete with much knowledge wholly new to him—which he will also find in Shakespeare.

A good example is this: Judge Webb proclaimed that in points of scientific lore (the lore of that age) Shakespeare and Bacon were much on a level. Professor Tyrrell, in a newspaper, said that the facts staggered him, as a "Stratfordian." A friend told me that he too was equally moved. I replied that these pseudoscientific "facts" had long been commonplaces. Pliny was a rich source of them. Professor Dowden took the matter up, with full knowledge,[64] and reconverted Mr. Tyrrell, who wrote: "I am not versed in the literature of the Shakespearian era, and I assumed that the Baconians who put forward the parallelisms had satisfied themselves that the coincidences were peculiar to the writings of the philosopher and the poet. Professor Dowden has proved that this is not so."[65]

---

[64] National Review, vol. xxxix., 1902.
[65] The Pilot, Aug. 30, 1902, p. 220.

Were I to enter seriously on this point of genius, I should begin by requesting my adversaries to read Mr. F. W. H. Myers's papers on "The Mechanism of Genius" (in his Human Personality), and to consider the humble problem of "Calculating Boys," which is touched on also by Cardinal Newman. How do they, at the age of innocence, arrive at their amazing results? How did the child Pascal, ignorant of Euclid, work out the Euclidean propositions of "bars and rounds," as he called lines and circles? Science has no solution!

Transport the problem into the region of poetry and knowledge of human nature, take Will in place of Pascal and Gauss, and (in manners and matter of war) Jeanne d'Arc;—and science, I fancy, is much to seek for a reply.

Mr. Greenwood considers, among others, the case of Robert Burns. The parallel is very interesting, and does not, I think, turn so much to Mr. Greenwood's advantage as he supposes. The genius of Burns, of course, is far indeed below the level of that of the author of the Shakespearean plays. But that author and Burns have this in common with each other (and obviously with Homer), that their work arises from a basis of older materials, already manipulated by earlier artists. Burns almost always has a key-note already touched, as confessedly in the poems of his predecessor, Fergusson; of Hamilton of Gilbertfield; in songs, popular or artistic, and so forth. He "alchemised" his materials, as Mr. Greenwood says of his author of the plays; turned dross into gold, brick into marble. Notoriously much Shakespearean work is of the same nature.

The education of Burns he owed to his peasant father, to his parish school (in many such schools he might have acquired Latin and Greek; in fact he did not), to a tutor who read with him some English and French; and he knew a modernised version of Blind Harry's Wallace; Locke's Essay; The Spectator, novels of the day, and vernacular Scots poets of his century, with a world of old Scots songs. These things, and such as these, were Burns's given literary materials. He used them in the only way open to him, in poems written for a rural audience, and published for an Edinburgh public. No classical, no theatrical materials were given; or, if he read the old drama, he could not, in his rural conditions, and in a Scotland where the theatre was in a very small way, venture on producing plays, for which there was no demand, while he had no knowledge of the Stage. Burns found and filled the only channels open to him, in a printed book, and in music books for which he transmuted old songs.

The bookish materials offered to Will, in London, were crammed with reminiscences from the classics, were mainly romantic and theatrical; and, from his profession of actor, by far the best channel open to him was the theatre. Badly as it paid the outside author, there was nothing that paid better. Venus and Adonis brought "more praise than pudding," if one may venture a guess. With the freedom of the theatre Will could soar to all heights and plumb all depths. No such opportunity had Burns, even if he could have used it, and, owing to a variety of causes, his spirit soon ceased to soar high or wing wide.

I take Shakespeare, in London at least, to have read the current Elizabethan light literature—Euphues, Lyly's Court comedies, novels full of the classics and of social life; Spenser, Sidney—his Defence of Poesy, and Arcadia (1590)—with scores of tales translated from the Italian, French, and Spanish, all full of foreign society, and discourses of knights and ladies. He saw the plays of the day, perhaps as one of "the groundlings." He often beheld Society, from without, when acting before the Queen and at great houses. He had thus, if I am right, sufficient examples of style and manner, and knowledge of how the great were supposed (in books) to comport and conduct themselves. The books were cheap, and could be borrowed, and turned over at the booksellers' stalls.[66] The Elizabethan style was omnipresent. Suppose that Shakespeare was a clever man, a lover of reading, a rapid reader with an excellent memory, easily influenced, like Burns, by what he read, and I really think that my conjectures are not too audacious. Not only "the man in the street," but "the reading public" (so loved by Coleridge), have not the beginning of a guess as to the way in which a quick man reads. Watch them poring for hours over a newspaper! Let me quote what Sir Walter Raleigh says:[67] "Shakespeare was one of those swift and masterly readers who know what they want of a book; they scorn nothing that is dressed in print, but turn over the pages with a quick discernment of all that brings them new information, or jumps with their thought, or tickles their fancy. Such a reader will have done with a volume in a few minutes, yet what he has taken from it he keeps for years. He is a live man; and is sometimes judged by slower wits to be a learned man."

I am taking Shakespeare to have been a reader of this kind, as was Dr. Johnson, as are not a few men who have no pretensions to genius. The accomplishment is only a marvel to—well, I need not be particular about the kind of person to whom it is a marvel!

Here, in fairness, the reader should be asked to consider an

---

[66] The oldest mention of a circulating library known to me is in Hull, in 1650, when Sir James Turner found it excellent.
[67] In his Shakespeare (English Men of Letters), pp. 66, 67.

eloquent passage of comparison between the knowledge of Burns and of Will, quoted by Mr. Greenwood[68] from Mr. Morgan.[69]

Genius, says Mr. Morgan, "did not guide Burns's untaught pen to write of Troy or Egypt, of Athens and Cyprus." No! that was not Burns's lay; nor would he have found a public had he emulated the contemporary St. Andrews professor, Mr. Wilkie, who wrote The Epigoniad, and sang of Cadmeian Thebes, to the delight of David Hume, his friend. The public of 1780–90 did not want new epics of heroic Greece from Mossgiel; nor was the literature accessible to Burns full of the mediæval legends of Troy and Athens. But the popular literature accessible to Will was full of the mediæval legends of Thebes, Troy, and Athens; and of these, not of Homer, Will made his market. Egypt he knew only in the new English version of Plutarch's Lives; of Homer, he (or the author of Troilus and Cressida) used only Iliad VII., in Chapman's new translation (1598). For the rest he had Lydgate (perhaps), and, certainly, Caxton's Destruction of Troy, still reprinted as a popular book as late as 1713. Will did not, as Mr. Morgan says, "reproduce the very counterfeit civilisations and manners of nations born and buried and passed into history a thousand years before he had been begotten... " He bestowed the manners of mediæval chivalrous romance on his Trojans and Greeks. He accommodated prehistoric Athens with a Duke. He gave Scotland cannon three hundred years too early; and made Cleopatra play at billiards. Look at his notion of "the very manners" of early post-Roman Britain in Cymbeline and King Lear! Concerning "the anomalous status of a King of Scotland under one of its primitive Kings" the author of Macbeth knew no more than what he read in Holinshed; of the actual truth concerning Duncan (that old prince was, in fact, a young man slain in a blacksmith's bothy), and of the whole affair, the author knew nothing but a tissue of sophisticated legends. The author of the plays had no knowledge (as Mr. Morgan inexplicably declares that he had) of "matters of curious and occult research for antiquaries or dilettanti to dig out of old romances or treaties or statutes rather than for historians to treat of or schools to teach!"

Mon Dieu! do historians not treat of "matters of curious research" and of statutes and of treaties? As for "old romances," they were current and popular. The "occult" sources of King Lear are a popular tale attached to legendary "history" and a story in Sidney's Arcadia. Will, whom Mr. Morgan describes as "a letterless peasant lad," or the Author, whoever he was, is not "invested with

---

[68] The Shakespeare Problem Restated, pp. 77, 78.
[69] The Shakespearean Myth, p. 162.

all the love" (sic, v.1. "lore"), "which the ages behind him had shut up in clasped books and buried and forgotten."

"Our friend's style has flowery components," Mr. Greenwood adds to this deliciously eloquent passage from his American author, "and yet Shakespeare who did all this," et cætera. But Shakespeare did not do "all this"! We know the sources of the plays well enough: novels in one of which "Delphos" is the insular seat of an oracle of Apollo; Holinshed, with his contaminated legends; North's Plutarch, done out of the French; older plays, and the rest of it. Shakespeare does not go to Tighernach and the Hennskringla for Macbeth; or for Hamlet to the saga which is the source of Saxo; or for his English chronicle-plays to the State Papers. Shakespeare did not, like William of Deloraine, dig up "clasped books, buried and forgotten." There is no original research; the author uses the romances, novels, ballads, and popular books of uncritical history which were current in his day. Mr. Greenwood knows that; Mr. Morgan, perhaps, knew it, but forgot what he knew; hurried away by the Muse of Eloquence. And the common Baconian may believe Mr. Morgan.

But Mr. Greenwood asks "what was the poetic output?" in Burns's case.[70] It was what we know, and that was what suited his age and his circumstances. It was lyric, idyll, song, and satire; it was not drama, for to the Stage he had no access, he who passed but one winter in Edinburgh, where the theatre was not the centre of literature.

Shakespeare came, with genius and with such materials as I have suggested, to an entirely different market, the Elizabethan theatre. I have tried to show how easily his mind might be steeped in the all-pervading classicism and foreign romance of the period, with the wide, sketchy, general information, the commonly known fragments from the great banquet of the classics,—with such history, wholly uncritical, as Holinshed and Stow, and other such English chroniclers, could copiously provide; with the courtly manners mirrored in scores of romances and Court plays; and in the current popular Morte d'Arthur and Destruction of Troy.

I can agree with Mr. Greenwood, when he says that "Genius is a potentiality, and whether it will ever become an actuality, and what it will produce, depends upon the moral qualities with which it is associated, and the opportunities that are open to it—in a word, on the circumstances of its environment."[71]

Of course by "moral qualities," a character without spot or

---

[70] The Shakespeare Problem Restated, p. 76.
[71] The Shakespeare Problem Restated, p. 81, note I.

stain is not intended: we may take that for granted. Otherwise, I agree; and think that Shakespeare of Stratford had genius, and that what it produced was in accordance with the opportunities open to it, and with "the circumstances of its environment." Without the "environment," no Jeanne d'Arc,—without the environment, no Shakespeare.

To come to his own, Shakespeare needed the environment of "the light people," the crowd of wits living from hand to mouth by literature, like Greene and Nash; and he needed that pell-mell of the productions of their pens: the novels, the poems, the pamphlets, and, above all, the plays, and the wine, the wild talk, the wit, the travellers' tales, the seamen's company, the vision of the Court, the gallants, the beauties; and he needed the People, of whom he does not speak in the terms of such a philanthropist as Bacon professedly was. Not as an aristocrat, a courtier, but as a simple literary man, William does not like, though he thoroughly understands, the mob. Like Alceste (in Le Misanthrope of Poquelin), he might say,

"L'Ami du genre humain n'est point du tout mon fait."

In London, not in Stratford, he could and did find his mob. This reminds one to ask, how did the Court-haunting, or the study-haunting, or law-court, and chamber of criminal examination-rooms haunting Bacon make acquaintance with Mrs. Quickly, and Doll Tearsheet, and drawers, and carters, and Bardolph, and Pistol, and copper captains, and all Shakespeare's crowd of people hanging loose on the town?

It is much easier to discover how Shakespeare found the tone and manners of courtly society (which, by the way, are purely poetic and conventional), than to find out where Bacon got his immense knowledge of what is called "low life."

If you reply, as regards Bacon, "his genius divined the Costards and Audreys, the Doll Tearsheets and tapsters, and drawers, and Bardolphs, and carters, from a hint or two, a glance," I answer that Will had much better sources for them in his own experience of life, and had conventional poetic sources for his courtiers—of whom, in the quick, he saw quite as much as Molière did of his Marquis.

But one Baconian has found out a more excellent way of accounting for Bacon's pictures of rude rustic life, and he is backed by Lord Penzance, that aged Judge. The way is short. These pictures of rural life and character were interpolated into the plays of Bacon by his collaborator, William Shakspere, actor, "who prepared the plays for the stage." This brilliant suggestion is borrowed from Mr. Appleton Morgan.[72]

Thus have these two Baconians perceived that it is difficult to see how Bacon obtained his knowledge of certain worlds and aspects of character which he could scarcely draw "from the life." I am willing to ascribe miracles to the genius of Bacon; but the Baconians cited give the honour to the actor, "who prepared the plays for the stage."

Take it as you please, my Baconian friends who do not believe as I believe in "Genius." Shakespeare and Molière did not live in "Society," though both rubbed shoulders with it, or looked at it over the invisible barrier between the actor and the great people in whose houses or palaces he takes the part of Entertainer. The rest they divined, by genius.

Bacon did not, perhaps, study the society of carters, drawers, Mrs. Quickly, and Doll Tearsheet; of copper captains and their boys; not at Court, not in the study, did he meet them. How then did he create his multitude of very low-lived persons? Rustics and rural constables he may have lovingly studied at Gorhambury, but for his collection of other very loose fish Bacon must have kept queer company. So you have to admit "Genius,"—the miracle of "Genius" in your Bacon,—to an even greater extent than I need it in the case of my Will; or, like Lord Penzance, you may suggest that Will collaborated with Bacon.

Try to imagine that Will was a born poet, like Burns, but with a very different genius, education, and environment. Burns could easily get at the Press, and be published: that was impossible for Shakespeare at Stratford, if he had written any lyrics. Suppose him to be a poet, an observer, a wit, a humorist. Tradition at Stratford says something about the humorist, and tradition, in similar circumstances, would have remembered no more of Burns, after the lapse of seventy years.

Imagine Will, then, to have the nature of a poet (that much I am obliged to assume), and for nine or ten years, after leaving school at thirteen, to hang about Stratford, observing nature and man, flowers and foibles, with thoughts incommunicable to Sturley and Quiney. Some sorts of park-palings, as he was married at eighteen, he could not break so lightly as Burns did,—some outlying deer he could not so readily shoot at, perhaps, but I am not surprised if he assailed other deer, and was in troubles many. Unlike Burns, he had a keen eye for the main chance. Everything

---

[72] Penzance, The Bacon-Shakespeare Controversy, pp. 150, 151. Citing Appleton Morgan's Shakespearean Myth, pp. 248, 298.

was going to ruin with his father; school-mastering, if he tried it (I merely follow tradition), was not satisfactory. His opinion of dominies, if he wrote the plays, was identical with that frequently expressed, in fiction and privately, by Sir Walter Scott.

Something must be done! Perhaps the straitest Baconian will not deny that companies of players visited Stratford, or even that he may have seen and talked with them, and been attracted. He was a practical man, and he made for London, and, by tradition, we first find him heading straight for the theatre, holding horses at the door, and organising a small brigade of boys as his deputies. According to Ben Jonson he shone in conversation; he was good company, despite his rustic accent, that terrible bar! The actors find that out; he is admitted within the house as a "servitor"—a call-boy, if you like; an apprentice, if you please.

By 1592, when Greene wrote his Groatsworth, "Shakescene" thinks he can bombast out a blank verse with the best; he is an actor, he is also an author, or a furbisher of older plays, and, as a member of the company, is a rival to be dreaded by Greene's three author friends: whoever they were, they were professional University playwrights; the critics think that Marlowe, so near his death, was one of them.

Will, supposing him to come upon the town in 1587, has now had, say, five years of such opportunities as were open to a man connected with the stage. Among these, in that age, we may, perhaps, reckon a good deal of very mixed society—writing men, bookish young blades, young blades who haunt the theatre, and sit on the stage, as was the custom of the gallants.

What follows? Chaff follows, a kind of intimacy, a supper, perhaps, after the play, if an actor seems to be good company. This is quite natural; the most modish young gallants are not so very dainty as to stand aloof from any amusing company. They found it among prize-fighters, when Byron was young, and extremely conscious of the fact that he was a lord. Moreover there were no women on the stage to distract the attention of the gallants. The players, says Asinius Lupus, in Jonson's Poetaster, "corrupt young gentry very much, I know it." I take the quotation from Mr. Greenwood.[73] They could not corrupt the young gentry, if they were not pretty intimate with them. From Ben's Poetaster, which bristles with envy of the players, Mr. Greenwood also quotes a railing address by a copper captain to Histrio, a poor actor, "There are some of you players honest, gentlemanlike scoundrels, and suspected to ha' some wit, as well as your poets, both at drinking

---

[73] The Shakespeare Problem Restated, p. 175.

and breaking of jests; and are companions for gallants. A man may skelder ye, now and then, of half a dozen shillings or so."[74] We think of Nigel Olifaunt in The Fortunes of Nigel; but better gallants might choose to have some acquaintance with Shakespeare.

To suppose that young men of position would not form a playhouse acquaintanceship with an amusing and interesting actor seems to me to show misunderstanding of human nature. The players were, when unprotected by men of rank, "vagabonds." The citizens of London, mainly Puritans, hated them mortally, but the young gallants were not Puritans. The Court patronised the actors who performed Masques in palaces and great houses. The wealth and splendid attire of the actors, their acquisition of land and of coats of arms infuriated the sweated playwrights. Envy of the actors appears in the Cambridge "Parnassus" plays of c. 1600–2. In the mouth of Will Kempe, who acted Dogberry in Shakespeare's company, and was in favour, says Heywood, with Queen Elizabeth, the Cambridge authors put this brag: "For Londoners, who of more report than Dick Burbage and Will Kempe? He is not counted a gentleman that knows not Dick Burbage and Will Kempe." It is not my opinion that Shakespeare was, as Ben Jonson came to be, as much "in Society" as is possible for a mere literary man. I do not, in fancy, see him wooing a Maid of Honour. He was a man's man, a peer might be interested in him as easily as in a jockey, a fencer, a tennis-player, a musician, que sçais-je? Southampton, discovering his qualities, may have been more interested, interested in a better way.

In such circumstances which are certainly in accordance with human nature, I suppose the actor to have been noticed by the young, handsome, popular Earl of Southampton; who found him interesting, and interested himself in the poet. There followed the dedication to the Earl of Venus and Adonis; a poem likely to please any young amorist (1693).

Mr. Greenwood cries out at the audacity of a player dedicating to an Earl, without even saying that he has asked leave to dedicate. The mere fact that the dedication was accepted, and followed by that of Lucrece, proves that the Earl did not share the surprise of Mr. Greenwood. He, conceivably, will argue that the Earl knew the real concealed author, and the secret of the pseudonym. But of the hypothesis of such a choice of a pseudonym, enough has been said. Whatever happened, whatever the Earl knew, if it were discreditable to be dedicated to by an actor, Southampton was discredited; for we

---

[74] The Shakespeare Problem Restated, p. 457.

are to prove that all in the world of letters and theatre who have left any notice of Shakespeare identified the actor with the poet.

This appears to me to be the natural way of looking at the affair. But, says Mr. Greenwood, of this intimacy or "patronage" of Southampton "not a scrap of evidence exists."[75] Where would Mr. Greenwood expect to find a scrap of evidence? In literary anecdote? Of contemporary literary anecdote about Shakespeare, as about Beaumont, Dekker, Chapman, Heywood, and Fletcher, there is none, or next to none. There is the tradition that Southampton gave the poet £1000 towards a purchase to which he had a mind. (Rowe seems to have got this from Davenant,—through Betterton.) In what documents would the critic expect to find a scrap of evidence? Perhaps in Southampton's book of his expenditure, and that does not exist. It is in the accounts of Prince Charlie that I find him, poor as he was, giving money to Jean Jacques Rousseau.

As to the chances of an actor's knowing "smart people," Heywood, who knew all that world, tells us[76] that "Tarleton, in his time, was gracious with the Queen, his sovereign," Queen Elizabeth. "Will Kempe was in the favour of his sovereign."

They had advantages, they were not literary men, but low comedians. I am not pretending that, though his

"flights upon the banks of Thames
So did take Eliza and our James,"

Will Shakspere "was gracious with the Queen."

We may compare the dedication of the Folio of 1623; here two players address the Earls of Pembroke and Montgomery. They have the audacity to say nothing about having asked and received permission to dedicate. They say that the Earls "have prosecuted both the plays and their authour living" (while in life) "with much favour." They "have collected and published the works of 'the dead' ... only to keep alive the memory of so worthy a Friend, and Fellow" (associate) "as was our Shakespeare, 'your servant Shakespeare.'"

Nothing can possibly be more explicit, both as to the actor's authorship of the plays, and as to the favour in which the two Earls held him. Mr. Greenwood[77] supposes that Jonson wrote the Preface, which contains an allusion to a well-known ode of Horace, and to a phrase of Pliny. Be that as it may, the Preface signed by the two players speaks to Pembroke and Montgomery. To them it cannot lie;

---

[75] The Shakespeare Problem Restated, p. 58.
[76] Apology the Actors, 1612.
[77] The Shakespeare Problem Restated, p. 267.

they know whether they patronised the actor or not; whether they believed, or not, that the plays were their "servant's." How is Mr. Greenwood to overcome this certain testimony of the Actors, to the identity of their late "Fellow" the player, with the author; and to the patronage which the Earls bestowed on him and his compositions? Mr. Greenwood says nothing except that we may reasonably suppose Ben to have written the dedication which the players signed.[78]

Whether or not the two Earls had a personal knowledge of Shakespeare, the dedication does not say in so many words. They had seen his plays and had "favoured" both him and them, with so much favour, had "used indulgence" to the author. That is not nearly explicit enough for the precise Baconians. But the Earls knew whether what was said were true or false. I am not sure whether the Baconians regard them as having been duped as to the authorship, or as fellow-conspirators with Ben in the great Baconian joke and mystery—that "William Shakespeare" the author is not the actor whose Stratford friend, Collyns, has his name written in legal documents as "William Shakespeare."

Anyone, however, may prefer to believe that, while William Shakspere was acting in a company (1592–3), Bacon, or who you please, wrote Venus and Adonis, and, signing "W. Shakspeare," dedicated it to his young friend, the Earl, promising to add "some graver labour," a promise fulfilled in Lucrece. In 1593, Bacon was chiefly occupied, we shall see, with the affairs of a young and beautiful Earl—the Earl of Essex, not of Southampton: to Essex he did not dedicate his two poems (if Venus and Lucrece were his). He "did nothing but ruminate" (he tells the world) on Essex. How Mr. Greenwood's Unknown was occupied in 1593–4, of course we cannot possibly be aware.

I have thus tried to show that Will Shakspere, if he had as much schooling as I suggest; and if he had four or five years of life in London, about the theatre, and, above all, had genius, might, by 1592, be the rising player-author alluded to as "Shakescene." There remains a difficulty. By 1592 Will had not time to be guilty of thirteen plays, or even of six. But I have not credited him with the authorship, between, say, 1587 and 1593, of eleven plays, namely, Hamlet, Romeo and Juliet, Midsummer Night's Dream, Titus Andronicus, Comedy of Errors, Love's Labour's Lost, King John, the three plays of Henry VI, and The Taming of the Shrew. Mr. Greenwood[79] cites Judge Webb for the fact that between the end of

---

[78] The Shakespeare Problem Restated, pp. 267, 268.
[79] The Shakespeare Problem Restated, pp. 50–52.

1587 and the end of 1592 "some half-dozen Shakespearean dramas had been written," and for Dr. Furnivall's opinion that eleven had been composed.

If I believed that half a dozen, or eleven Shakespearean plays, as we have them, had been written or composed, between 1587 and 1592, I should be obliged to say that, in my opinion, they were not composed, in these five years, by Will. Mr. Greenwood writes, "Some of the dates are disputable"; and, for himself, would omit "Titus Andronicus, the three plays of Henry VI, and possibly also The Taming of the Shrew, while the reference to Hamlet also is, as I have elsewhere shown, of very doubtful force."[80] This leaves us with six of Dr. Furnivall's list of earliest plays put out of action. The miracle is decomposing, but plays numerous enough to stagger my credulity remain.

I cannot believe that the author even of the five plays before 1592–3 was the ex-butcher's boy. Meanwhile these five plays, written by somebody before 1593, meet the reader on the threshold of Mr. Greenwood's book[81] with Dr. Furnivall's eleven; and they fairly frighten him, if he be a "Stratfordian." "Will, even Will," says the Stratfordian, "could not have composed the five, much less the eleven, much less Mr. Edwin Reed's thirteen 'before 1592.'"[82] But, at the close of his work[83] Mr. Greenwood reviews and disbands that unlucky troop of thirteen Shakespearean plays "before 1592" as mustered by Mr. Reed, a Baconian of whom Mr. Collins wrote in terms worthy of feu Mr. Bludyer of The Tomahawk.

From the five plays left to Shakespeare's account in p. 51, King John (as we know it) is now eliminated. "I find it impossible to believe that the same man was the author of the drama" (The Troublesome Reign of King John) "published in 1591, and that which, so far as we know, first saw the light in the Folio of 1623 ... Hardly a single line of the original version reappears in the King John of Shakespeare."[84] "I think it is a mistake to endeavour to fortify the argument against him" (my Will, toi que j'aime), "by ascribing to Shakespeare such old plays as the King John of 1591 or the primitive Hamlet."[85]

I thought so too, when I read p. 51, and saw King John

---

[80] The Shakespeare Problem Restated, p. 51.
[81] The Shakespeare Problem Restated, p. 51.
[82] Ibid., p. 500, citing Mr. Reed's Francis Bacon our Shake-speare, chap. ii. pp. 62, 63.
[83] Ibid., pp. 500–520, chap xvi.
[84] The Shakespeare Problem Restated, p. 512.
[85] Ibid., p. 514.

apparently still "coloured on the card" among "Shakespeare's lot." We are now left with Love's Labour's Lost, Midsummer Night's Dream, Comedy of Errors, and Romeo and Juliet, out of Dr. Furnivall's list of plays up to 1593. The phantom force of miraculously early plays is "following darkness like a dream." We do not know the date of A Midsummer Night's Dream, we do not know the date of Romeo and Juliet. Mr. Gollancz dates the former "about 1592," and the latter "at 1591."[86] This is a mere personal speculation. Of Love's Labour's Lost, we only know that our version is one "corrected and augmented" by William Shakespeare in 1598. I dare say it is as early as 1591–2, in its older form. Of The Comedy of Errors, Mr. Collins wrote, "It is all but certain that it was written between 1589 and 1592, and it is quite certain that it was written before the end of 1594."[87]

The legion of Shakespearean plays of date before 1593 has vanished. The miracle is very considerably abated. In place of introducing the airy hosts of plays before 1592, in p. 51, it would have been, perhaps, more instructive to write that, as far as we can calculate, Shakespeare's earliest trials of his pinions as a dramatist may be placed about 1591–3. There would then have been no specious appearance of miracles to be credited by Stratfordians to Will. But even so, we have sufficient to "give us pause," says Mr. Greenwood, with justice. It gives me "pause," if I am to believe that, between 1587 and 1592, Will wrote Love's Labour's Lost, The Comedy of Errors, A Midsummer Night's Dream, and Romeo and Juliet. There is a limit even to my gullibility, and if anyone wrote all these plays, as we now possess them, before 1593, I do not suppose that Will was the man. But the dates, in fact, are unknown: the miracle is apocryphal.

---

[86] Ibid., p. 386, note I.
[87] Ibid., p. 93.

VI

THE COURTLY PLAYS: "LOVE'S LABOUR'S LOST"

We now come to consider another "miracle" discovered in the plays,—a miracle if the actor be the author. The new portent is the courtliness and refinement (too often, alas! the noblest ladies make the coarsest jokes) and wit of the speeches of the noble gentlemen and ladies in the plays. To be sure the refinement in the jests is often conspicuously absent. How could the rude actor learn his quips and pretty phrases, and farfetched conceits? This question I have tried to answer already,—the whole of these fashions abound in the literature of the day.

Here let us get rid of the assumption that a poet could not make the ladies and gentlemen of his plays converse as they do converse, whether in quips and airs and graces, or in loftier style, unless he himself frequented their society. Marlowe did not frequent the best society; he was no courtier, but there is the high courtly style in the speeches of the great and noble in Edward II. Courtiers and kings never did speak in this manner, any more than they spoke in blank verse. The style is a poetical convention, while the quips and conceits, the airs and graces, ran riot through the literature of the age of Lyly and his Euphues and his comedies, the age of the Arcadia.

A cheap and probable source of Will's courtliness is to be found in the courtly comedies of John Lyly, five of which were separately printed between 1584 and 1592. Lyly's "real significance is that he was the first to bring together on the English stage the elements of high comedy, thereby preparing the way for Shakespeare's Much Ado about Nothing and As You Like It" (and Love's Labour's Lost, one may add). "Whoever knows his Shakespeare and his Lyly well can hardly miss the many evidences that Shakespeare had read Lyly's plays almost as closely as Lyly had read Pliny's Natural History... . One could hardly imagine Love's Labour's Lost as existent in the period from 1590 to 1600, had not Lyly's work just preceded it."[88]

"It is to Lyly's plays," writes Dr. Landmann, "that Shakespeare

---

[88] Cambridge History of English Literature, vol. v. p. 126. Prof. G. P. Baker.

owes so much in the liveliness of his dialogues, in smartness of expression, and especially in that predilection for witticisms, quibbles, and playing upon words which he shows in his comedies as well as in his tragedies." There follows a dissertation on the affected styles of Guevara and Gongora, of the Pléiade in France, and generally of the artificial manner in Europe, till in England we reach Lyly, "in whose comedies," says Dr. Furness, "I think we should look for motives which appeared later in Shakespeare."[89]

The Baconians who think that a poet could not derive from books and court plays his knowledge of fashions far more prevalent in literature than at Court, decide that the poet of Love's Labour's Lost was not Will, but the courtly "concealed poet." No doubt Baconians may argue with Mr. R. M. Theobald[90] that "Bacon wrote Marlowe," and, by parity of reasoning many urge, though Mr. Theobald does not, that Bacon wrote Lyly, pouring into Lyly's comedies the grace and wit, the quips and conceits of his own courtly youth. "What for no?" The hypothesis is as good as the other hypotheses, "Bacon wrote Marlowe," "Bacon wrote Shakespeare."

The less impulsive Baconians and the Anti-Willians appear to ignore the well-known affected novels which were open to all the world, and are noted even in short educational histories of English literature. Shakespeare, in London, had only to look at the books on the stalls, to read or, if he had the chance, to see Lyly's plays, and read the poems of the time. I am taking him not to be a dullard but a poet. It was not hard for him, if he were a poet of genius, not only to catch the manner of Lyly's Court comedies, and "Marlowe's mighty line" (Marlowe was not "brought up on the knees of Marchionesses"!), but to improve on them. People did not commonly talk in the poetical way, heaven knows; people did not write in the poetic convention. Certainly Queen Mary and Queen Elizabeth talked and wrote, as a rule (we have abundance of their letters), like women of this world. There is a curious exception in Letter VIII of the Casket Letters from Mary to Bothwell. In this (we have a copy of the original French), Mary plunges into the affected and figured style already practised by Les Précieuses of her day; and expands into symbolisms in a fantastic jargon. If courtiers of both sexes conversed in the style of Euphues (which is improbable), they learned the trick of it from Euphues; not the author of Euphues from them. Lyly's most popular prose was accessible to

---

[89] Furness, Love's Labour's Lost, pp. xiii., 348–350: cf. pp. 348, 349, for the four distinct styles of linguistic affectation of the period, at least as they are represented in literature.
[90] Shakespeare Studies in Baconian Light, Appendix on Marlowe.

Shakespeare. The whole convention as to how the great should speak and bear themselves was accessible in poetry and the drama. A man of genius naturally made his ladies and courtiers more witty, more "conceited," more eloquent, more gracious than any human beings ever were anywhere, in daily life.

It seems scarcely credible that one should be obliged to urge facts so obvious against the Baconian argument that only a Bacon, intimately familiar with the society of the great, could make the great speak as, in the plays, they do—and as in real life they probably did not!

We now look at Love's Labour's Lost, published in quarto, in 1598, as "corrected and augmented by W. Shakespere." The date of composition is unknown, but the many varieties of versification, with some allusions, mark it as among the earliest of the dramas. Supposing that Shakespeare obtained his knowledge of fine manners and speech, and of the tedious quips and conceits which he satirises, from the contemporary poems, plays, and novels which abounded in them, and from précieux and précieuses who imitated them, as I suggest, even then Love's Labour's Lost is an extremely eccentric piece. I cannot imagine how a man who knew the foreign politics of his age as Bacon did, could have dreamed of writing anything so eccentric, that is, if it has any connection with foreign politics of the time.

The scene is the Court of Ferdinand, King of Navarre. In 1589–93, the eyes of England were fixed on the Court of her ally, Henri of Navarre, in his struggle with the League and the Guises; the War of Religion. But the poet calls the King "Ferdinand," taking perhaps from some story this non-existent son of Charles III of Navarre (died 1425): to whom, according to Monstrelet, the Burgundian chronicler of that time, the French king owed 200,000 ducats of gold. This is a transaction of the early fifteenth century, and leads to the presence of the princess of France as an envoy at the Court of Navarre in the play; the whole thing is quite unhistorical, and has the air of being borrowed from some lost story or brief novel. Bacon's brother, Anthony, was English minister at the Court of Navarre. What could tempt Bacon to pick out a non-historical King Ferdinand of Navarre, plant him in the distant days of Jeanne d'Arc, and make him, at that period, found an Academe for three years of austere study and absence of women? But, if Bacon did this, what could induce him to give to the non-existent Ferdinand, as companions, the Maréchal de Biron with de Longueville (both of them, in 1589–93, the chief adherents of Henri of Navarre), and add to them "Dumain," that is, the Duc de Mayenne, one of the Guises, the deadly foes of Henri and of the

Huguenots? Even in the unhistorically minded Shakespeare, the freak is of the most eccentric,—but in Bacon this friskiness is indeed strange. I cannot, like Mr. Greenwood,[91] find any "allusions to the Civil War of France." France and Navarre, in the play, are in full peace.

The actual date of the fabulous King Ferdinand would have been about 1430. By introducing Biron, Longueville, and the Duc de Mayenne, and Bankes's celebrated educated horse, the author shifts the date to 1591. But the Navarre of the play is a region "out of space, out of time," a fairy world of projected Academes (like that of the four young men in de la Primaudaye's L'Académie Française, Englished in 1586) and of eace, while the actual King of Navarre of 1591 was engaged in a struggle for life and faith; and in his ceaseless amours.

Many of Shakespeare's anachronisms are easily intelligible. He takes a novel or story about any remote period, or he chooses, as for the Midsummer Night's Dream, a period earlier than that of the Trojan war. He gives to the Athens contemporary with the "Late Minoan III" period (1600 B.C.?) a Duke, and his personages live like English nobles and rustics of his own day, among the fairies of English folk-lore. It is the manner of Chaucer and of the poets and painters of any age before the end of the eighteenth century. The resulting anachronisms are natural and intelligible. We do not expect war-chariots in Troilus and Cressida; it is when the author makes the bronze-clad Achæans familiar with Plato and Aristotle that we are surprised. In Love's Labour's Lost we do not expect the author to introduce the manners of the early fifteenth century, the date of the affair of the 200,000 ducats. Let the play reflect the men and manners of 1589–93,—but why place Mayenne, a fanatical Catholic foe of Navarre, among the courtiers of the Huguenot King of Navarre?

As for de Mayenne (under the English spelling of the day Dumain) appearing as a courtier of his hated adversary Henri, Bacon, of all men, could not have made that absurd error. It was Shakespeare who took but an absent-minded interest in foreign politics. If Bacon is building his play on an affair, the ducats, of 1425–35 (roughly speaking), he should not bring in a performing horse, trained by Bankes, a Staffordshire man, which was performing its tricks at Shrewsbury—in 1591.[92] Thus early we find that great scholar mixing up chronology in a way which, in

---

[91] The Shakespeare Problem Restated, p. 516.
[92] Act i. Scene 2. Furness, Love's Labour's Lost, p. 45, note.

Shakespeare even, surprises; but, in Bacon, seems quite out of keeping.

Shakespeare, as Sir Sidney Lee says, gives Mayenne as "Dumain,"—Mayenne, "whose name was so frequently mentioned in popular accounts of French affairs in connection with Navarre's movements that Shakespeare was led to number him also among his supporters." Bacon would not have been so led! As Mayenne and Henri fought against each other at Ivry, in 1590, this was carrying nonsense far, even for Will, but for the earnestly instructive Bacon!

"The habits of the author could not have been more scholastic," so Judge Webb is quoted, "if he had, like Bacon, spent three years in the University of Cambridge..." Bacon, or whoever corrected the play in 1598, might have corrected "primater" into "pia mater," unless Bacon intended the blunder for a malapropism of "Nathaniel, a Curate." Either Will or Bacon, either in fun or ignorance, makes Nathaniel turn a common Italian proverb on Venice into gibberish. It was familiar in Florio's Second Frutes (1591), and First Frutes (1578), with the English translation. The books were as accessible to Shakspere as to Bacon. Either author might also draw from James Sandford's Garden of Pleasure, done out of the Italian in 1573–6.

Where the scholastic habits of Bacon at Cambridge are to be discovered in this play, I know not, unless it be in Biron's witty speech against study. If the wit implies in the author a Cambridge education, Costard and Dull and Holofernes imply familiarity with rustics and country schoolmasters. Where the author proves that he "could not have been more familiar with French politics if, like Bacon, he had spent three years in the train of an Ambassador to France," I cannot conjecture. There are no French politics in the piece, any more than there are "mysteries of fashionable life," such as Bacon might have heard of from Essex and Southampton. There is no "familiarity with all the gossip of the Court"; there is no greater knowledge of foreign proverbs than could be got from common English books. There is abundance, indeed overabundance of ridicule of affected styles, and quips, with which the literature of the day was crammed: call it Gongorism, Euphuism, or what you please. One does not understand how or where Judge Webb (in extreme old age) made all these discoveries, sympathetically quoted by Mr. Greenwood.[93] "Like Bacon, the author of the play must have had a large command of books; he must have had his "Horace," his "Ovidius Naso," and his "good old 'Mantuan.'" What a prodigious "command of books"! Country schoolmasters confessedly had these

---

[93] The Shakespeare Problem Restated, pp. 67, 68.

books on the school desks. It was not even necessary for the author to "have access to the Chronicles of Monstrelet." It is not known, we have said, whether or not such plot as the play possesses, with King Ferdinand and the 100,000 ducats, or 200,000 ducats (needed to bring the Princess and the mythical King Ferdinand of Navarre together), were not adapted by the poet from an undiscovered conte, partly based on a passage in Monstrelet.

Perhaps it will be conceded that Love's Labour's Lost is not a play which can easily be attributed to Bacon. We do not know how much of the play existed before Shakespeare "augmented" it in 1598. We do not know whether what he then corrected and augmented was an early work of his own or from another hand, though probably it was his own. Molière certainly corrected and augmented and transfigured, in his illustrious career in Paris, several of the brief early sketches which he had written when he was the chief of a strolling troupe in Southern France.

Mr. Greenwood does not attribute the wit (such as it is), the quips, the conceits, the affectations satirised in Love's Labour's Lost, to Will's knowledge of the artificial style then prevalent in all the literatures of Western Europe, and in England most pleasingly used in Lyly's comedies. No, "the author must have been not only a man of high intellectual culture, but one who was intimately acquainted with the ways of the Court, and the fashionable society of his time, as also with contemporary foreign politics."[94]

I search the play once more for the faintest hint of knowledge of foreign politics. The embassy of the daughter of the King of France (who, by the date of the affair of the ducats, should be Charles VII) has been compared to a diplomatic sally of the mother of the childless actual King of France (Henri III), in 1586, when Catherine de Medici was no chicken. I do not see in the embassy of the Princess of the story any "intimate acquaintance with contemporary foreign politics" about 1591–3. The introduction of Mayenne as an adherent of the King of Navarre, shows either a most confused ignorance of foreign politics on the part of the author, or a freakish contempt for his public. I am not aware that the author shows any "intimate acquaintance with the ways" of Elizabeth's Court, or of any other fashionable society, except the Courts which Fancy held in plays.

Mr. Greenwood[95] appears to be repeating "the case as to this very remarkable play" as "well summed up by the late Judge Webb in his Mystery of William Shakespeare" (p. 44). In that paralysing

---

[94] The Shakespeare Problem Restated, p. 66.
[95] Ibid., p. 67.

judicial summary, as we have seen, "the author could not have been more familiar with French politics if, like Bacon, he had spent three years in the train of an Ambassador to France." The French politics, in the play, are to send the daughter of a King of France (the contemporary King Henri III was childless) to conduct a negotiation about 200,000 ducats, at the Court, steeped in peace, of a King of Navarre, a scholar who would fain be a recluse from women, in an Academe of his own device. Such was not the Navarre of Henri in his war with the Guises, and Henri did not shun the sex!

Such are the "contemporary foreign politics," the "French politics" which the author knows—as intimately as Bacon might have known them. They are not foreign politics, they are not French politics, they are politics of fairy-land: with which Will was at least as familiar as Bacon.

These, then, are the arguments in favour of Bacon, or the Great Unknown, which are offered with perfect solemnity of assurance: and the Baconians repeat them in their little books of popularisation and propaganda. Quantula sapientia!

VII

CONTEMPORARY RECOGNITION OF WILL AS AUTHOR

It is absolutely impossible to prove that Will, or Bacon, or the Man in the Moon, was the author of the Shakespearean plays and poems. But it is easy to prove that Will was recognised as the author, by Ben Jonson, Heywood, and Heminge and Condell the actors, to take the best witnesses. Meanwhile we have received no hint that any man except Will was ever suspected of being the author till 1856, when the twin stars of Miss Delia Bacon and Mr. Smith arose. The evidence of Ben Jonson and the rest can only prove that professed playwrights and actors, who knew Will both on and off the stage, saw nothing in him not compatible with his work. Had he been the kind of letterless country fellow, or bookless fellow whom the Baconians and Mr. Greenwood describe, the contemporary witnesses cited must have detected Will in a day; and the story of the "Concealed Poet" who really, at first, did the additions and changes in the Company's older manuscript plays, and of the inconceivably impudent pretences of Will of Stratford, would have kept the town merry for a month. Five or six threadbare scholars would have sat down at a long table in a tavern room, and, after their manner, dashed off a Comedy of Errors on the real and the false playwright.

Baconians never seem to think of the mechanical difficulties in their assumed literary hoax. If Will, like the old Hermit of Prague who never saw pen and ink, could not even write, the hoax was a physical impossibility. If he could write, but was a rough bookless man, his condition would be scarcely the more gracious, even if he were able to copy in his scrawl the fine Roman hand of the concealed poet. I am surprised that the Baconians have never made that point. Will's "copy" was almost without blot or erasion, the other actors were wont to boast. Really the absence of erasions and corrections is too easily explained on the theory that Will was not the author. Will merely copied the fair copies handed to him by the concealed poet. The farce was played for some twenty years, and was either undetected or all concerned kept the dread secret—and all the other companies and rival authors were concerned in exposing the imposture.

The whole story is like the dream of a child. We therefore expect the Anti-Willians to endeavour to disable the evidence of

Jonson, Heywood, Heminge, and Condell. Their attempts take the shape of the most extravagant and complex conjectures; with certain petty objections to Ben's various estimates of the merits of the plays. He is constant in his witness to the authorship. To these efforts of despair we return later, when we hope to justify what is here deliberately advanced.

Meanwhile we study Mr. Greenwood's attempts to destroy or weaken the testimony of contemporary literary allusions, in prose or verse, to the plays as the work of the actor. Mr. Greenwood rests on an argument which perhaps could only have occurred to legal minds, originally, perhaps to the mind of Judge Webb, not in the prime vigour of his faculties. Not very many literary allusions remain, made during Will's life-time, to the plays of Shakespeare. The writers, usually, speak of "Shakespeare," or "W. Shakespeare," or "Will Shakespeare," and leave it there. In the same way, when they speak of other contemporaries, they name them,—and leave it there, without telling us "who" (Frank) Beaumont, or (Kit) Marlowe, or (Robin) Greene, or (Jack) Fletcher, or any of the others "were." All interested readers knew who they were: and also knew who "Shakespeare" or "Will Shakespeare" was. No other Will Shak(&c.) was prominently before the literary and dramatic world, in 1592–1616, except the Warwickshire provincial who played with Burbage.

But though the mere names of the poets, Ben Jonson, Kit Marlowe, Frank Beaumont, Harry Chettle, and so forth, are accepted as indicating the well-known men whom they designate, this evidence to identity does not satisfy Mr. Greenwood, and the Baconians, where Will is concerned. "We should expect to find allusions to dramatic and poetical works published under the name of 'Shakespeare'; we should expect to find Shakespeare spoken of as a poet and a dramatist; we should expect, further, to find some few allusions to Shakespeare or Shakspere the player. And these, of course, we do find; but these are not the objects of our quest. What we require is evidence to establish the identity of the player with the poet and dramatist; to prove that the player was the author of the Plays and Poems. That is the proposition to be established, and that the allusions fail, as it appears to me, to prove," says Mr. Greenwood. He adds, "At any rate they do not disprove the theory that the true authorship was hidden under a pseudonym"[96] —which raises an entirely different question.

Makers of allusions to the plays must identify Shakespeare with the actor, explicitly; must tell us who this Shakespeare was, though they need not, and usually do not, tell us who the other

---

[96] The Shakespeare Problem Restated, p. 307.

authors mentioned were; and though the world of letters and the Stage knew but one William Shakspere or Shakespeare, who was far too familiar to them to require further identification. But even if the makers of allusions did all this, and said, "by W. Shakespeare the poet, we mean W. Shakespeare the actor"—that is not enough. For they may all be deceived, may all believe that a bookless, untutored man is the author. So we cannot get evidence correct enough for Mr. Greenwood.

Destitute as I am of legal training, I leave this notable way of disposing of the evidence to the judgement of the Bench and the Bar, a layman intermeddleth not with it. Still, I am, like other readers, on the Jury addressed,—I do not accept the arguments. Miror magis, as Mr. Greenwood might quote Latin. We have already seen one example of this argument, when Heywood speaks of the author of poems by Shakespeare, published in The Passionate Pilgrim. Heywood does nothing to identify the actor Shakspere with the author Shakespeare, says Mr. Greenwood. I shall prove that, elsewhere, Heywood does identify them, and no man knew more of the world of playwrights and actors than Heywood. I add that in his remarks on The Passionate Pilgrim, Heywood had no need to say "by W. Shakespeare I mean the well-known actor in the King's Company." There was no other William Shakspere or Shakespeare known to his public.

It is to no purpose that Mr. Greenwood denies, as we have seen above, that the allusions "disprove the theory that the true authorship was hidden under a pseudonym." That is an entirely different question. He is now starting quite another hare. Men of letters who alluded to the plays and poems of William Shakespeare, meant the actor; that is my position. That they may all have been mistaken: that "William Shakespeare" was Bacon's, or any one's pseudonym, is, I repeat, a wholly different question; and we must not allow the critic to glide away into it through an "at any rate"; as he does three or four times. So far, then, Mr. Greenwood's theory that it was impossible for the actor Shakspere to have been the author of the plays, encounters the difficulty that no contemporary attributed them to any other hand: that none is known to have said, "This Warwickshire man cannot be the author."

"Let us, however, examine some of these allusions to Shakspere, real or supposed," says the critic.[97] He begins with the hackneyed words of the dying man of letters, Robert Greene, in A Groatsworth of Wit (1592). The pamphlet is addressed to Gentlemen of his acquaintance "that spend their wits in making

---

[97] The Shakespeare Problem Restated, p. 308.

plays"; he "wisheth them a better exercise," and better fortunes than his own. (Marlowe is supposed to be one of the three Gentlemen playwrights, but such suppositions do not here concern us.) Greene's is the ancient feud between the players and the authors, between capital and labour. The players are the capitalists, and buy the plays out and out,—cheap. The author has no royalties; and no control over the future of his work, which a Shakspere or a Bacon, a Jonson or a Chettle, or any handyman of the company owning the play, may alter as he pleases. It is highly probable that the actors also acquired most of the popular renown, for, even now, playgoers have much to say about the players in a piece, while they seldom know the name of the playwright. Women fall in love with the actors, not with the authors; but with "those puppets," as Greene says, "that speake from our mouths, these anticks, garnished in our colours." Ben Jonson, we shall see, makes some of the same complaints,—most natural in the circumstances: though he managed to retain the control of his dramas; how, I do not know. Greene adds that in his misfortunes, illness, and poverty, he is ungratefully "forsaken," by the players, and warns his friends that such may be their lot; advising them to seek "some better exercise." He then writes—and his meaning cannot easily be misunderstood, I think, but misunderstood it has been—"Yes, trust them not" (trust not the players), "FOR there is an upstart crow, beautified with our feathers, that with his Tyger's heart wrapt in a Player's hide" ("Player's" in place of "woman's," in an old play, The Tragedy of Richard, Duke of York, &c.), "supposes he is as well able to bumbast out a blank verse as the best of you; and being an absolute Johannes Factotum, is in his own conceit the only Shake-scene in a country."

The meaning is pellucid. "Do not trust the players, my fellow playwrights, for the reasons already given, for they, in addition to their glory gained by mouthing our words, and their ingratitude, may now forsake you for one of themselves, a player, who thinks his blank verse as good as the best of yours" (including Marlowe's, probably). "The man is ready at their call" ("an absolute Johannes Factotum"). "In his own conceit" he is "the only Shake-scene in a country." "Seek you better masters," than these players, who have now an author among themselves, "the only Shake-scene," where the pun on Shakespeare does not look like a fortuitous coincidence. But it may be, anything may happen.

The sense, I repeat, is pellucid. But Mr. Greenwood writes that if Shake-scene be an allusion to Shakespeare "it seems clear that it is as an actor rather than as an author he is attacked."[98] As an

---

[98] The Shakespeare Problem Restated, p. 309.

actor the person alluded to is merely assailed with the other actors, his "fellows." But he is picked out as presenting another and a new reason why authors should distrust the players, "for there is" among themselves, "in a player's hide," "an upstart crow"—who thinks his blank verse as good as the best of theirs. He is, therefore, necessarily a playwright, and being a factotum, can readily be employed by the players to the prejudice of Greene's three friends, who are professed playwrights.

Mr. Greenwood says that "we do not know why Greene should have been so particularly bitter against the players, and why he should have thought it necessary so seriously to warn his fellow playwrights against them."[99] But we cannot help knowing; for Greene has told us. In addition to gaining renown solely through mouthing "our" words, wearing "our feathers," they have been bitterly ungrateful to Greene in his poverty and sickness; they will, in the same circumstances, as cruelly forsake his friends; "yes, for they now have" an author, and to the playwrights a dangerous rival, in their own fellowship. Thus we know with absolute certainty why Greene wrote as he did. He says nothing about the superior financial gains of the players, which Mr. Greenwood suspects to have been the "only" cause of his bitterness. Greene gives its causes in the plainest possible terms, as did Ben Jonson later, in his verses "Poet-Ape" (Playwright-Actor). Moreover, Mr. Greenwood gives Greene's obvious motives on the very page where he says that we do not know them.

Even Mr. Greenwood,[100] anxious as he is to prove Shake-scene to be attacked as an actor, admits that the words "supposes himself as well able to bumbast out a blank verse as the best of you," "do seem to have that implication,"[101] namely, that "Shake-scene" is a dramatic author: what else can the words mean; why, if not for the Stage, should Shake-scene write blank verse?

Finally Mr. Greenwood, after saying "it is clear that it is as an actor rather than as an author that 'Shake-scene' is attacked,"[102] concedes[103] that it "certainly looks as if he" (Greene) "meant to suggest that this Shake-scene supposed himself able to compose, as well as to mouth verses." Nothing else can possibly be meant. "The rest of you" were authors, not actors.

If not, why, in a whole company of actors, should "Shake-

---

[99] The Shakespeare Problem Restated, p. 310.
[100] Ibid., pp. 310, 311.
[101] Ibid., p. 311.
[102] The Shakespeare Problem Restated, p. 309.
[103] Ibid., pp. 311, 312.

scene" alone be selected for a special victim? Shake-scene is chosen out because, as an author, a factotum always ready at need, he is more apt than the professed playwrights to be employed as author by his company: this is a new reason for not trusting the players.

I am not going to take the trouble to argue as to whether, in the circumstances of the case, "Shake-scene" is meant by Greene for a pun on "Shake-speare," or not. If he had some other rising player-author, the Factotum of a cry of players, in his mind, Baconians may search for that personage in the records of the stage. That other player-author may have died young, or faded into obscurity. The term "the only Shake-scene" may be one of those curious coincidences which do occur. The presumption lies rather on the other side. I demur, when Mr. Greenwood courageously struggling for his case says that, even assuming the validity of the surmise that there is an allusion to Shakspere,[104] "the utmost that we should be entitled to say is that Greene here accuses Player Shakspere of putting forward, as his own, some work, or perhaps some parts of a work, for which he was really indebted to another" (the Great Unknown?). I do more than demur, I defy any man to exhibit that sense in Greene's words.

"The utmost that we should be entitled to say," is, in my opinion, what we have no shadow of a title to say. Look at the poor hackneyed, tortured words of Greene again. "Yes, trust them not; for there is an upstart crow, beautified with our feathers, that with his Tyger's heart wrapped in a player's hide, supposes he is as well able to bumbast out a blank verse as the best of you; and being an absolute Johannes Factotum, is in his own conceit the only Shake-scene in a country."

How can mortal man squeeze from these words the charge that "Player Shakspere" is "putting forward, as his own, some work, or perhaps some parts of a work, for which he was really indebted to another"? It is as an actor, with other actors, that the player is "beautified with our feathers,"—not with the feathers of some one not ourselves, Bacon or Mr. Greenwood's Unknown. Mr. Greenwood even says that Shake-scene is referred to "as beautified with the feathers which he has stolen from the dramatic writers" ("our feathers").

Greene says absolutely nothing about feathers "which he has stolen." The "feathers," the words of the plays, were bought, not stolen, by the actors, "anticks garnished in our colours."

Tedious it is to write many words about words so few and simple as those of Greene; meaning "do not trust the players, for

---

[104] The Shakespeare Problem Restated, pp. 312, 313.

one of them writes blank verse which he thinks as good as the best of yours, and fancies himself the only Shake-scene in a country."

But "Greene here accuses Player Shakspere of putting forward, as his own, some work, or perhaps some parts of a work, for which he was really indebted to another," this is "the utmost we should be entitled to say," even if the allusion be to Shakspere. How does Mr. Greenwood get the Anti-Willian hypothesis out of Greene's few and plain words?

It is much safer for him to say that "Shake-scene" is not meant for Shakespeare. Nobody can prove that it is; the pun may be a strange coincidence,—or any one may say that he thinks it nothing more; if he pleases.

Greene nowhere "refers to this Shake-scene as being an impostor, an upstart crow beautified with the feathers which he has stolen from the dramatic writers ("our feathers")"[105] —that is, Greene makes no such reference to Shake-scene in his capacity of writer of blank verse. Like all players, who are all "anticks garnisht in our colours," Shake-scene, as player, is "beautified with our feathers." It is Mr. Greenwood who adds "beautified with the feathers which he has stolen from the dramatic writers." Greene does not even remotely hint at plagiarism on the part of Shake-scene: and the feathers, the plays of Greene and his friends, were not stolen but bought. We must take Greene's evidence as we find it,—it proves that by "Shake-scene" he means a "poet-ape," a playwright-actor; for Greene, like Jonson, speaks of actors as "apes." Both men saw in a certain actor and dramatist a suspected rival. Only one such successful practising actor-playwright is known to us at this date (1592–1601),—and he is Shakespeare. Unless another such existed, Greene, in 1592, alludes to William Shak(&c.) as a player and playwright. This proves that the actor from Stratford was accepted in Greene's world as an author of plays in blank verse. He cannot, therefore, have seemed incapable of his poetry.

Let us now briefly consider other contemporary allusions to Shakespeare selected by Mr. Greenwood himself. No allusion can prove that Shakespeare was the author of the work attributed to him in the allusions. The plays and poems may have been by James VI and I, "a parcel-poet." The allusions can prove no more than that, by his contemporaries, Shakespeare was believed to be the poet, which is impossible if he were a mere rustic ignoramus, as the Baconians aver. Omitting some remarks by Chettle on Greene's Groatsworth of Wit,[106] as, if grammar goes for all, they do not refer to Shakespeare,

---

[105] The Shakespeare Problem Restated, p. 313.
[106] See Appendix II, "Chettle's supposed allusion to Will Shakspere."

we have the Cambridge farce or comedy on contemporary literature, the Return from Parnassus (1602?). The University wits laugh at Shakespeare,—not an university man, as the favourite poet, in his Venus and Adonis, of a silly braggart pretender to literature, Gullio.

They also introduce Kempe, the low comedy man of Shakespeare's company, speaking to Burbage, the chief tragic actor, of Shakespeare as a member of their company, who, as an author of plays, "puts down" the University wits "and Ben Jonson too." The date is not earlier than that of Ben's satiric play on the poets, The Poetaster (1601), to which reference is made. Since Kempe is to be represented as wholly ignorant, his opinion of Shakespeare's pre-eminent merit only proves, as in the case of Gullio, that the University wits decried the excellences of Shakespeare. In him they saw no scholar.

The point is that Kempe recognises Shakespeare as both actor and author.

All this "is quite consistent with the theory that Shake-speare was a pseudonym,"[107] says Mr. Greenwood. Of course it is, but it is not consistent with the theory that Shakespeare was an uneducated, bookless rustic, for, in that case, his mask would have fallen off in a day, in an hour. Of course the Cambridge author only proves, if you will, that he thought that Kempe thought, that his fellow player was the author. But we have better evidence of what the actors thought than in the Cambridge play.

In 1598, as we saw, Francis Meres in Palladis Tamia credits Shakespeare with Venus and Adonis, with privately circulated sonnets, and with a number of the comedies and tragedies. How the allusions "negative the hypothesis that Shakespeare was a nom de plume is not apparent," says Mr. Greenwood, always constant to his method. I repeat that he wanders from the point, which is, here, that the only William Shak(&c.) known to us at the time, in London, was credited with the plays and poems on all sides, which proves that no incompatibility between the man and the works was recognised.

Then Weaver (1599) alludes to him as author of Venus, Lucrece, Romeo, Richard, "more whose names I know not." Davies (1610) calls him "our English Terence" (the famous comedian), and mentions him as having "played some Kingly parts in sport." Freeman (1614) credits him with Venus and Lucrece. "Besides in plays thy wit winds like Meander." I repeat Heywood's evidence. Thomas Heywood, author of that remarkable domestic play, A Woman Killed with Kindness, was, from the old days of Henslowe,

---

[107] The Shakespeare Problem Restated, p. 330.

in the fifteen-nineties, a playwright and an actor; he survived into the reign of Charles I. Writing on the familiar names of the poets, "Jack Fletcher," "Frank Beaumont," "Kit Marlowe," "Tom Nash," he says,

> "Mellifluous Shakespeare whose enchanting quill
> Commanded mirth and passion, was but 'Will.'"

Does Heywood not identify the actor with the author? No quibbles serve against the evidence.

We need not pursue the allusions later than Shakespeare's death, or invoke, at present, Ben Jonson's panegyric of 1623. As to Davies, his dull and obscure epigram is addressed "To our English Terence, Mr. Will Shake-speare." He accosts Shakespeare as "Good Will." He remarks that, "as some say," if Will "had not played some Kingly parts in sport," he had been "a companion for a King," and "been a King among the meaner sort." Nobody, now, can see the allusion and the joke. Shakespeare's company, in 1604, acted a play on the Gowrie Conspiracy of 1600. King James suppressed the play after the second night, as, of course, he was brought on the stage throughout the action: and in very droll and dreadful situations. Did Will take the King's part, and annoy gentle King Jamie, "as some say"? Nobody knows. But Mr. Greenwood, to disable Davies's recognition of Mr. Will as a playwright, "Our English Terence," quotes, from Florio's Montaigne, a silly old piece of Roman literary gossip, Terence's plays were written by Scipio and Laelius. In fact, Terence alludes in his prologue to the Adelphi, to a spiteful report that he was aided by great persons. The prologue may be the source of the fable—that does not matter. Davies might get the fable in Montaigne, and, knowing that some Great One wrote Will's plays, might therefore, in irony, address him as "Our English Terence." This is a pretty free conjecture! In Roman comedy he had only two names known to him to choose from; he took Terence, not Plautus. But if Davies was in the great Secret, a world of others must have shared le Secret de Polichinelle. Yet none hints at it, and only a very weak cause could catch at so tiny a straw as the off-chance that Davies knew, and used "Terence" as a gibe.[108]

The allusions, even the few selected, cannot prove that the actor wrote the plays, but do prove that he was believed to have done so, and therefore that he was not so ignorant and bookless as to demonstrate that he was incapable of the poetry and the

---

[108] The Vindicators of Shakespeare, pp. 115, 116, 211. See my Introduction, p. xxii.

knowledge displayed in his works. Mr. Greenwood himself observes that a Baconian critic goes too far when he makes Will incapable of writing. Such a Will could deceive no mortal.[109] But does Mr. Greenwood, who finds in the Author of the plays "much learning, and remarkable classical attainments," or "a wide familiarity with the classics,"[110] suppose that his absolutely bookless Will could have persuaded his intimates that he was the author of plays exhibiting "a wide familiarity with the classics," or "remarkable classical attainments." The thing is wholly impossible.

I do not remember that a single contemporary allusion to Shakespeare speaks of him as "learned," erudite, scholarly, and so forth. The epithets for him are "sweet," "gentle," "honeyed," "sugared," "honey-tongued"—this is the convention. The tradition followed by Milton, who was eight years of age when Shakespeare died, and who wrote L'Allegro just after leaving Cambridge, makes Shakespeare "sweetest Shakespeare, Fancy's child," with "native wood-notes wild"; and gives to Jonson "the learned sock." Fuller, like Milton, was born eight years before the death of Shakespeare, namely, in 1608. Like Milton he was a Cambridge man. The First Folio of Shakespeare's works appeared when each of these two bookish men was aged fifteen. It would necessarily revive interest in Shakespeare, now first known as far as about half of his plays went: he would be discussed among lovers of literature at Cambridge. Mr. Greenwood quotes Fuller's remark that Shakespeare's "learning was very little," that, if alive, he would confess himself "to be never any scholar."[111] I cannot grant that Fuller is dividing the persons of actor and author. Men of Shakespeare's generation, such as Jonson, did not think him learned; nor did men of the next generation. If Mr. Collins's view be correct, the men of Shakespeare's and of Milton's generations were too ignorant to perceive that Shakespeare was deeply learned in the literature of Rome, and in the literature of Greece. Every one was too ignorant, till Mr. Collins came.

---

[109] The Vindicators of Shakespeare, p. 210.
[110] Ibid., p. 136.
[111] The Shakespeare Problem Restated, p. 338.

VIII

"THE SILENCE OF PHILIP HENSLOWE"

When Shakespeare is mentioned as an author by contemporary writers, the Baconian stratagem, we have seen, is to cry, "Ah, but you cannot prove the author mentioned to be the actor." We have seen that Meres (1598) speaks of Shakespeare as the leading tragic and comic poet ("Poor poet-ape that would be thought our chief," quoth Jonson), as author of Venus and Adonis, and as a sonneteer. "All this does nothing whatever to support the idea that the Stratford player was the author of the plays and poems alluded to," says Mr. Greenwood, playing that card again.[112]

The allusions, I repeat, do prove that Shak(&c.), the actor, was believed to be the author, till any other noted William Shak(&c.) is found to have been conspicuously before the town. "There is nothing at all to prove that Meres, native of Lincolnshire, had any personal knowledge of Shakespeare." There is nothing at all to prove that Meres, native of Lincolnshire, had any personal knowledge of nine-tenths of the English authors, famous or forgotten, whom he mentions. "On the question—who was Shakespeare?—he throws no light." He "throws no light on the question" "who was?" any of the poets mentioned by him, except one, quite forgotten, whose College he names ... To myself this "sad repeated air,"—"critics who praise Shakespeare do not say who Shakespeare was,"—would appear to be, not an argument, but a subterfuge: though Mr. Greenwood honestly believes it to be an argument,—otherwise he would not use it: much less would he repeat it with frequent iteration. The more a man was notorious, as was Will Shakspere the actor, the less the need for any critic to tell his public "who Shakespeare was."

As Mr. Greenwood tries to disable the evidence when Shakespeare is alluded to as an author, so he tries to better his case when, in the account-book of Philip Henslowe, an owner of theatres, money-lender, pawn-broker, purchaser of plays from authors, and so forth, Shakespeare is not mentioned at all. Here is a mystery which, properly handled, may advance the great cause. Henslowe has notes of loans of money to several actors, some of them of Shakespeare's company, "The Lord Chamberlain's." There is no such note of a loan to Shakespeare. Does this prove that he was not

---

[112] The Shakespeare Problem Restated, p. 346.

an actor? If so, Burbage was not an actor; Henslowe never names him.

There are notes of payments of money to Henslowe after each performance of any play in one of his theatres. In these notes the name of Shakespeare is never once mentioned as the author of any play. How weird! But in these notes the names of the authors of the plays acted are never mentioned. Does this suggest that Bacon wrote all these plays?

On the other hand, there are frequent mentions of advances of money to authors who were working at plays for Henslowe, singly, or in pairs, threes, fours, or fives. We find Drayton, Dekker, Chapman, and nine authors now forgotten by all but antiquarians. We have also Ben Jonson (1597), Marston, Munday, Middleton, Webster, and others, authors in Henslowe's pay. But the same of Shakespeare never appears. Mysterious! The other men's names, writes Dr. Furness, occur "because they were all writers for Henslowe's theatre, but we must wait at all events for the discovery of some other similar record, before we can produce corresponding memoranda regarding Shaksper" (sic) "and his productions."[113]

The natural mind of the ordinary man explains all by saying, "Henslowe records no loans of money to Shakspere the actor, because he lent him no money. He records no payments for plays to Shakespeare the author-actor, because to Henslowe the actor sold no plays." That is the whole explanation of the Silence of Philip Henslowe. If Shakspere did sell a play to Henslowe, why should that financier omit the fact from his accounts? Suppose that the actor was illiterate as Baconians fervently believe, and sold Bacon's plays, what prevented him from selling a play of Bacon's (under his own name, as usual) to Henslowe? To obtain a Baconian reply you must wander into conjecture, and imagine that Bacon forbade the transaction. Then why did he forbid it? Because he could get a better price from Shakspere's company? The same cause would produce the same effect on Shakspere himself; whether he were the author, or were Bacon's, or any man's go-between. On any score but that of money, why was Henslowe good enough for Ben Jonson, Dekker, Heywood, Middleton, and Webster, and not good enough for Bacon, who did not appear in the matter at all, but was represented in it by the actor, Will? As a gentleman and a man of the Court, Bacon would be as much discredited if he were known to sell (for £6 on an average) his noble works to the Lord Chamberlain's Company, as if he sold them to Henslowe.

I know not whether the great lawyer, courtier, scholar, and

---

[113] Cited in The Shakespeare Problem Restated, p. 353.

philosopher is supposed by Baconians to have given Will Shakspere a commission on his sales of plays; or to have let him keep the whole sum in each case. I know not whether the players paid Shakspere a sum down for his (or Bacon's) plays, or whether Will received a double share, or other, or any share of the profits on them, as Henslowe did when he let a house to the players. Nobody knows any of these things.

"If Shakspere the player had been a dramatist, surely Henslowe would have employed him also, like the others, in that behalf."[114] Henslowe would, if he could have got the "copy" cheap enough. Was any one of "the others," the playwrights, a player, holding a share in his company? If not, the fact makes an essential difference, for Shakspere was a shareholder. Collier, in his preface to Henslowe's so-called "Diary," mentions a playwright who was bound to scribble for Henslowe only (Henry Porter), and another, Chettle, who was bound to write only for the company protected by the Earl of Nottingham.[115] Modern publishers and managers sometimes make the same terms with novelists and playwrights.

It appears to me that Shakspere's company would be likely, as his plays were very popular, to make the same sort of agreement with him, and to give him such terms as he would be glad to accept,—whether the wares were his own—or Bacon's. He was a keen man of business. In such a case, he would not write for Henslowe's pittance. He had a better market. The plays, whether written by himself, or Bacon, or the Man in the Moon, were at his disposal, and he did not dispose of them to Henslowe, wherefore Henslowe cannot mention him in his accounts. That is all.

Quoting an American Judge (Dr. Stotsenburg, apparently), Mr. Greenwood cites the circumstance that, in two volumes of Alleyn's papers "there is not one mention of such a poet as William Shaksper in his list of actors, poets, and theatrical comrades."[116] If this means that Shakspere is not mentioned by Alleyn among actors, are we to infer that William was not an actor? Even Baconians insist that he was an actor. "How strange, how more than strange," cries Mr. Greenwood, "that Henslowe should make no mention in all this long diary, embracing all the time from 1591 to 1609, of the actor-author ... No matter. Credo quia impossibile!"[117] Credo what? and what is impossible? Henslowe's volume is no Diary; he does not tell a single anecdote of any description; he merely enters loans, gains, payments. Does Henslowe mention, say,

---

[114] The Shakespeare Problem Restated, p. 353.
[115] Diary, pp. xxvii, xxviii.
[116] The Shakespeare Problem Restated, p. 367.
[117] Ibid., pp. 368, 369.

Ben Jonson, when he is not doing business with Ben? Does he mention any actor or author except in connection with money matters? Then, if he did no business with Shakspere the actor, in borrowing or lending, and did no business with Shakespeare the author, in borrowing, lending, buying or selling, "How strange, how more than strange" it would be if Henslowe did mention Shakespeare! He was not keeping a journal of literary and dramatic jottings. He was keeping an account of his expenses and receipts. He never names Richard Burbage any more than he mentions Shakespeare.

Mr. Greenwood again expresses his views about this dark suspicious mystery, the absence of Shakespeare or Shakspere (or Shak, as you like it), from Henslowe's accounts, if Shak(&c.) wrote plays. But the mystery, if mystery there be, is just as obscure if the actor were the channel through which Bacon's plays reached the stage, for the pretended author of these masterpieces. Shak—was not the man to do all the troking, bargaining, lying, going here and there, and making himself a motley to the view for £0, 0s. 0d. If he were a sham, a figure-head, a liar, a fetcher-and-carrier of manuscripts, he would be paid for it. But he did not deal with Henslowe in his bargainings, and that is why Henslowe does not mention him. Mr. Greenwood, in one place,[118] agrees, so far, with me. "Why did Henslowe not mention Shakespeare as the writer of other plays" (than Titus Andronicus and Henry VI)? "I think the answer is simple enough." (So do I.) "Neither Shakspere nor 'Shakespeare' ever wrote for Henslowe!" The obvious is perceived at last; and the reason given is "that he was above Henslowe's 'skyline,'" "he" being the Author. We only differ as to why the author was above Henslowe's "sky-line." I say, because good Will had a better market, that of his Company. I understand Mr. Greenwood to think,—because the Great Unknown was too great a man to deal with Henslowe. If to write for the stage were discreditable, to deal (unknown) with Henslowe was no more disgraceful than to deal with "a cry of players"; and as (unknown) Will did the bargaining, the Great Unknown was as safe with Will in one case as in the other. If Will did not receive anything for the plays from his own company (who firmly believed in his authorship), they must have said, "Will! dost thou serve the Muses and thy obliged fellows for naught? Dost thou give us two popular plays yearly,—gratis?"

Do you not see that, in the interests of the Great Secret itself, Will had to take the pay for the plays (pretended his) from somebody. Will Shakspere making his dear fellows and friends a

---

[118] The Shakespeare Problem Restated, p. 354.

present of two masterpieces yearly was too incredible. So I suppose he did have royalties on the receipts, or otherwise got his money; and, as he certainly did not get them from Henslowe, Henslowe had no conceivable reason for entering Will's name in his accounts.

Such are the reflections of a plain man, but to an imaginative soul there seems to be a brooding mist, with a heart of fire, which half conceals and half reveals the darkened chamber wherein abides "The Silence of Philip Henslowe." "The Silence of Philip Henslowe," Mr. Greenwood writes, "is a very remarkable phenomenon..." It is a phenomenon precisely as remarkable as the absence of Mr. Greenwood's name from the accounts of a boot-maker with whom he has never had any dealings.

"If, however, there was a man in high position, 'a concealed poet,'" who "took the works of others and rewrote and transformed them, besides bringing out original plays of his own ... then it is natural enough that his name should not appear among those [of the] for the most part impecunious dramatists to whom Henslowe paid money for playwriting."[119] Nothing can be more natural, and, in fact, the name of Bacon, or Southampton, or James VI, or Sir John Ramsay, or Sir Walter Raleigh, or Sir Fulke Greville, or any other "man in high position," does not appear in Henslowe's accounts. Nor does the name of William Shak(&c.). But why should it not appear if Will sold either his own plays, or those of the noble friend to whom he lent his name and personality—to Henslowe? Why not?

Then consider the figure, to my mind impossible, of the great "concealed poet" "of high position," who can "bring out original plays of his own," and yet "takes the works of others," say of "sporting Kyd," or of Dekker and Chettle, and such poor devils,—takes them as a Yankee pirate-publisher takes my rhymes,—and "rewrites and transforms them."

Bacon (or Bungay) cannot "take" them without permission of their legal owners,—Shakspere's or any other company;—of any one, in short, who, as Ben Jonson says, "buys up reversions of old plays." How is he to manage these shabby dealings? Apparently he employs Will Shakspere, spells his own "nom de plume" "Shakespeare," and has his rewritings and transformations of the destitute author's work acted by Will's company. What a situation for Bacon, or Sir Fulke Greville, or James VI, or any "man in high position" whom fancy can suggest! The plays by the original authors, whoever they were, could only be obtained by the "concealed poet" and "man in high position" from the legal owners, Shakspere's company, usually. The concealed poet had to negotiate with the owners, and Bacon (or

---

[119] The Shakespeare Problem Restated, p. 366.

whoever he was) employed that scamp Will Shakspere, first, I think, to extract the plays from the owners, and then to pretend that he himself, even Will, had "rewritten and transformed them."

What an associate was our Will for the concealed poet; how certain it was that Will would blackmail the "man in high position"! "Doubtless" he did: we find Bacon arrested for debt, more than once, while Will buys New Place, in Stratford, with the money extorted from the concealed poet of high position.[120] Bacon did associate with that serpent Phillips, a reptile of Walsingham, who forged a postscript to Mary Stuart's letter to Babington. But now, if not Bacon, then some other concealed poet of high position, with a mysterious passion for rewriting and transforming plays by sad, needy authors, is in close contact with Will Shakspere, the Warwickshire poacher and ignorant butcher's boy, country schoolmaster, draper's apprentice, enfin, tout le tremblement.

"How strange, how more than strange!"

The sum of the matter seems to me to be that from as early as March 3, 1591, we find Henslowe receiving small sums of money for the performances of many plays. He was paid as owner or lessee of the House used by this or that company. On March 3, 1591, the play acted by "Lord Strange's (Derby's) men" was Henry VI. Several other plays with names familiar in Shakespeare's Works, such as Titus Andronicus, all the three parts of Henry VI, King Leare (April 6, 1593), Henry V (May 14, 1592), The Taming of a Shrew (June 11, 1594), and Hamlet, paid toll to Henslowe. He "received" so much, on each occasion, when they were acted in a theatre of his. But he never records his purchase of these plays; and it is not generally believed that Shakespeare was the author of all these plays, in the form which they bore in 1591–4: though there is much difference of opinion.

There is one rather interesting case. On August 25, 1594, Henslowe enters "ne" (that is, "a new play") "Received at the Venesyon Comodey, eighteen pence." That was his share of the receipts. The Lord Chamberlain's Company, that of Shakespeare, was playing in Henslowe's theatre at Newington Butts. If the "Venesyon Comodey" (Venetian Comedy) were The Merchant of Venice, this is the first mention of it. But nobody knows what Henslowe meant by "the Venesyon Comodey." He does not mention the author's name, because, in this part of his accounts he never does mention the author or authors. He only names them when he buys from, or lends to, or has other money dealings with the authors. He had none with Shakespeare, hence the Silence of Philip Henslowe.

---

[120] Some Baconians say so!

IX

THE LATER LIFE OF SHAKESPEARE—HIS MONUMENT AND PORTRAITS

In the chapter on the Preoccupations of Bacon the reader may find help in making up his mind as to whether Bacon, with his many and onerous duties and occupations, his scientific studies, and his absorbing scientific preoccupation, is a probable author of the Shakespearean plays. Mr. Greenwood finds the young Shakspere impossible—because of his ignorance—which made him such a really good pseudo-author, and such a successful mask for Bacon, or Bacon's unknown equivalent. The Shakspere of later life, the well-to-do Shakspere, the purchaser of the right to bear arms; so bad at paying one debt at least; so eager a creditor; a would-be encloser of a common; a man totally bookless, is, to Mr. Greenwood's mind, an impossible author of the later plays.

Here, first, are moral objections on the ground of character as revealed in some legal documents concerning business. Now, I am very ready to confess that William's dealings with his debtors, and with one creditor, are wholly unlike what I should expect from the author of the plays. Moreover, the conduct of Shelley in regard to his wife was, in my opinion, very mean and cruel, and the last thing that we could have expected from one who, in verse, was such a tender philanthropist, and in life was—women apart—the best-hearted of men. The conduct of Robert Burns, alas, too often disappoints the lover of his Cottar's Saturday Night and other moral pieces. He was an inconsistent walker.

I sincerely wish that Shakespeare had been less hard in money matters, just as I wish that in financial matters Scott had been more like himself, that he had not done the last things that we should have expected him to do. As a member of the Scottish Bar it was inconsistent with his honour to be the secret proprietor of a publishing and a printing business. This is the unexplained moral paradox in the career of a man of chivalrous honour and strict probity: but the fault did not prevent Scott from writing his novels and poems. Why, then, should the few bare records of Shakspere's monetary transactions make his authorship impossible? The objection seems weakly sentimental.

Macaulay scolds Scott as fiercely as Mr. Greenwood scolds Shakspere,—for the more part, ignorantly and unjustly. Still, there is matter to cause surprise and regret. Both Scott and Shakspere are accused of writing for gain, and of spending money on lands and houses with the desire to found families. But in the mysterious mixture of each human personality, any sober soul who reflects on his own sins and failings will not think other men's failings incompatible with intellectual excellence. Bacon's own conduct in money matters was that of a man equally grasping and extravagant. Ben Jonson thus describes Shakespeare as a social character: "He was indeed honest, and of an open and free nature ... I loved the man and do honour his memory on this side idolatry as much as any." Perhaps Ben never owed money to Shakspere and refused to pay!

We must not judge a man's whole intellectual character, and declare him to be incapable of poetry, on the score of a few legal papers about matters of business. Apparently Shakspere helped that Elizabethan Mr. Micawber, his father, out of a pecuniary slough of despond, in which the ex-High Bailiff of the town was floundering,— pursued by the distraint of one of the friendly family of Quiney— Adrian Quiney. They were neighbours and made a common dunghill in Henley Street.[121] I do not, like Mr. Greenwood, see anything "at all out of the way" in the circumstance "that a man should be writing Hamlet, and at the same time bringing actions for petty sums lent on loan at some unspecified interest."[122] Nor do I see anything at all out of the way in Bacon's prosecution of his friend and benefactor, Essex (1601), while Bacon was writing Hamlet. Indeed, Shakspere's case is the less "out of the way" of the two. He wanted his loan to be repaid, and told his lawyer to bring an action. Bacon wanted to keep his head (of inestimable value) on his shoulders; or to keep his body out of the Tower; or he merely, as he declares, wanted to do his duty as a lawyer of the Crown. In any case, Bacon was in a tragic position almost unexampled; and was at once overwhelmed by work, and, one must suppose, by acute distress of mind, in the case of Essex. He must have felt this the more keenly, if, as some Baconians vow, he wrote the Sonnets to Essex. Whether he were writing his Hamlet when engaged in Essex's case (1601), or any other of his dramatic masterpieces, even this astonishing man must have been sorely bestead to combine so many branches of business.

Thus I would reply to Mr. Greenwood's amazement that Shakspere, a hard creditor, and so forth, should none the less have been able to write his plays. But if it is meant that a few business transactions must have absorbed the whole consciousness of

---

[121] The Shakespeare Problem Restated, pp. 181, 397.
[122] Ibid., p. 186.

Shakespeare, and left him neither time nor inclination for poetry, consider the scientific preoccupation of Bacon, his parliamentary duties, his ceaseless activity as "one of the legal body-guard of the Queen" at a time when he had often to be examining persons accused of conspiracy,—and do not forget his long and poignant anxiety about Essex, his constant efforts to reconcile him with Elizabeth, and to advocate his cause without losing her favour; and, finally, the anguish of prosecuting his friend, and of knowing how hardly the world judged his own conduct. Follow him into his relations with James I; his eager pursuit of favour, the multiplicity of his affairs, his pecuniary distresses, and the profound study and severe labour entailed by the preparation for and the composition of The Advancement of Learning (1603–5). He must be a stout-hearted Baconian who can believe that, between 1599 and 1605, Bacon was writing Hamlet, and other masterpieces of tragedy or comedy. But all is possible to genius. What Mr. Greenwood's Great Unknown was doing at this period, "neither does he know, nor do I know, but he only." He, no doubt, had abundance of leisure.

At last Shakspere died (1616), and had not the mead of one melodious tear, as far as we know, from the London wits, in the shape of obituary verses. This fills Mr. Greenwood with amazement. "Was it because 'the friends of the Muses' were for the most part aware that Shakespeare had not died with Shakspere?" Did Jonson perchance think that his idea might be realised when he wrote,

"What a sight it were,
To see thee in our waters yet appear"?

and so on. Did Jonson expect and hope to see the genuine "Shakespeare" return to the stage, seven years after the death of Shakspere the actor, the Swan of Avon? As Jonson was fairly sane, we can no more suspect him of having hoped for this miracle than believe that most of the poets knew the actor not to be the author. Moreover Jonson, while desiring that Shakespeare might "shine forth" again and cheer the drooping stage, added,

"Which since thy flight from hence hath mourned like Night,
And despairs day, but for thy volume's light,"

that is—the Folio of 1623. Ben did not weave the amazing tissue of involved and contradictory falsities attributed to him by Baconians. Beaumont died in the same year as Shakspere, who died in the depths of the country, weary of London. Has Mr. Greenwood found obituary poems dropped on the grave of the famous Beaumont? Did

Fletcher, did Jonson, produce one melodious tear for the loss of their friend; in Fletcher's case his constant partner? No? Were the poets, then, aware that Beaumont was a humbug, whose poems and plays were written by Bacon?[123]

I am not to discuss Shakespeare's Will, the "second-best bed," and so forth. But as Shakespeare's Will says not a word about his books, it is decided by Mr. Greenwood that he had no books. Mr. Greenwood is a lawyer; so was my late friend Mr. Charles Elton, Q.C., of White Staunton, who remarks that Shakespeare bequeathed "all the rest of my goods, chattels, leases, &c., to my son-in-law, John Hall, gent." (He really was a "gent." with authentic coat-armour.)

It is with Mr. Elton's opinion, not with my ignorance, that Mr. Greenwood must argue in proof of the view that "goods" are necessarily exclusive of books, for Mr. Elton takes it as a quite natural fact that Shakespeare's books passed, with his other goods, to Mr. Hall, and thence to a Mr. Nash, to whom Mr. Hall left "my study of books"[124] (library). I only give this as a lawyer's opinion.

There is in the Bodleian an Aldine Ovid, "with Shakespeare's" signature (merely Wm. She.), and a note, "This little volume of Ovid was given to me by W. Hall, who sayd it was once Will Shakespeare's." I do not know that the signature (like that on Florio's Montaigne, in the British Museum) has been detected as a forgery; nor do I know that Shakespeare's not specially mentioning his books proves that he had none. Lawyers appear to differ as to this inference: both Mr. Elton and Mr. Greenwood seem equally confident.[125] But if it were perfectly natural that the actor, Shakspere, should have no books, then he certainly made no effort, by the local colour of owning a few volumes, to persuade mankind that he was the author. Yet they believed that he was—really there is no wriggling out of it. As regards any of his own MSS. which Shakespeare may have had (one would expect them to be at his theatre), and their monetary value, if they were not, as usual, the property of his company, and of him as a member thereof, we can discuss that question in the section headed "The First Folio."

---

[123] Some verses of Fletcher's may, perhaps, refer to Beaumont's death.
[124] C. I. Elton, Shakespeare, His Family and Friends, pp. 246, 247.
[125] As to the Aldine Ovid in the Bodleian, see Mr. Greenwood in The Vindicators of Shakespeare, pp. 191, 192. Of course he raises every objection, but I do not feel sure that either an affirmative or negative result can be attained by expertise. We are not told when or where the Bodleian obtained the book; nor what is the date of the handwriting of the inscription about W. Hall, a personage whom we are to meet later. A good deal of business is done in forging names in books.

It appears that Shakespeare's daughter, Judith, could write no more than her grandfather.[126] Nor, I repeat, could the Lady Jane Gordon, daughter of the great Earl of Huntly, when she was married to the Earl of Bothwell in 1566. At all events, Lady Jane "made her mark." It may be feared that Judith, brought up in that very illiterate town of Stratford, under an illiterate mother, was neglected in her education. Sad, but very common in women of her rank, and scarcely a proof that her father did not write the plays.

As "nothing is known of the disposition and character"[127] of Shakespeare's grand-daughter, Lady Barnard, who died in 1670, it is not so paralysingly strange that nothing is known of any relics or anecdotes of Shakespeare which she may have possessed. Mr. Greenwood "would have supposed that she would have had much to say about the great poet," exhibited his books (if any), and so forth. Perhaps she did,—but how, if we "know nothing about her disposition and character," can we tell? No interviewers rushed to her house (Abington Hall, Northampton-shire) with pencils and notebooks to record her utterances; no reporter interviewed her for the press. It is surprising, is it not?

The inference might be drawn, in the Baconian manner, that, during the Commonwealth and Restoration, "the friends of the Muses" knew that the actor was not the author, and therefore did not interview his granddaughter in the country.

"But, at any rate, we have the Stratford monument," says Mr. Greenwood, and delves into this problem. Even the Stratford monument of Shakespeare in the parish church is haunted by Baconian mysteries. If the gentle reader will throw his eye over the photograph[128] of the monument as it now exists, he may not be able to say to the face of the poet—

> "Thou wast that all to me, Will,
> For which my soul did pine."

But if he has any knowledge of Jacobean busts on monuments, he will probably agree with me in saying, "This effigy, though executed by somebody who was not a Pheidias, and who perhaps worked merely from descriptions, is, at all events, Jacobean." The same may assuredly be said of the monument; it is in good Jacobean style: the pillars with their capitals are graceful: all the rest is in keeping; and the two inscriptions are in the square

---

[126] The Shakespeare Problem Restated, p. 196.
[127] Ibid., p. 197.
[128] See Frontispiece.

capital letters of inscriptions of the period; not in italic characters. Distrusting my own expertise, I have consulted Sir Sidney Colvin, and Mr. Holmes of the National Portrait Gallery. They, with Mr. Spielmann, think the work to be of the early seventeenth century.

Next, glance at the figure opposite. This is a reproduction of "the earliest representation of the Bust" (and monument) in Dugdale's Antiquities of Warwickshire (1656). Compare the two objects, point by point, from the potato on top with holes in it, of Dugdale, which is meant for a skull, through all the details,—bust and all. Does Dugdale's print, whether engraved by Hollar or not, represent a Jacobean work? Look at the two ludicrous children, their legs dangling in air; at the lions' heads above the capitals of the pillars; at the lettering of the two visible words of the inscription, and at the gloomy hypochondriac or lunatic, clasping a cushion to his abdomen. That hideous design was not executed by an artist who "had his eye on the object," if the object were a Jacobean monument: while the actual monument was fashioned in no period of art but the Jacobean. From Digges' rhymes in the Folio of 1623, we know that Shakespeare already had his "Stratford monument." The existing object is what he had; the monument in Dugdale is what, I hope, no architect of 1616–23 could have imagined or designed.

Dugdale's engraving is not a correct copy of any genuine Jacobean work of art. Is Dugdale accurate in his reproductions of other monuments in Stratford Church? To satisfy himself on this point, Sir George Trevelyan, as he wrote to me (June 13, 1912), "made a sketch of the Carew Renaissance monument in Stratford Church, and found that the discrepancies between the original tomb and the representation in Dugdale's Warwickshire are far and away greater than in the monument to William Shakespeare."

Mr. Greenwood,[129] while justly observing that "the little sitting figures ... are placed as no monumental sculptor would place them," "on the whole sees no reason at all why we should doubt the substantial accuracy of Dugdale's figure ... It is impossible to suppose that Hollar would have drawn and that Dugdale would have published a mere travesty of the Stratford Monument."

I do not know who drew the design, but a travesty of Jacobean work it is in every detail of the monument. A travesty is what Dugdale gives as a representation of the Carew monument. Mr. Greenwood, elsewhere, repeating his criticism of the impossible figures of children, says: "This is certainly mere matter of detail, and, in the absence of other evidence, would give us no warrant for

---

[129] The Shakespeare Problem Restated, pp. 247, 248, note I.

doubting the substantial accuracy of Dugdale's presentment of the 'Shakespeare' bust."[130]

Why are we to believe that Dugdale's artist was merely fantastic in his design of the children (and also remote from Jacobean taste in every detail), and yet to credit him with "substantial accuracy" in his half-length of a gloomy creature clutching a cushion to his stomach? With his inaccuracies as to the Carew monument, why are we to accept him as accurate in his representation of the bust? Moreover, other evidence is not wanting. It is positively certain that the monument existing in 1748, was then known as "the original monument," and that no other monument was put in its place, at that date or later.

Now Mrs. Stopes[131] argues that in 1748 the monument was "entirely reconstructed," and so must have become no longer what Dugdale's man drew, but what we see to-day. It is positively certain that her opinion is erroneous.

If ever what we see to-day was substituted for anything like what Dugdale's man drew, the date of the substitution is unknown.

Mrs. Stopes herself discovered the documents which disprove her theory. They were known to Halliwell-Phillipps, who quotes an unnamed "contemporary account."[132] This account Mrs. Stopes, with her tireless industry, found in the Wheler manuscripts, among papers of the Rev. Joseph Greene, in 1746 Head Master of the Grammar School. In one paper of September 1740 "the original monument" is said to be "much impaired and decayed." There was a scheme for making "a new monument" in Westminster Abbey. That, I venture to think, would have been in Hanoverian, not in Jacobean taste and style. But there was no money for a new monument. Mrs. Stopes also found a paper of November 20, 1748, showing that in September 1746, Mr. Ward (grandfather of Mrs. Siddons) was at Stratford with "a cry of players." He devoted the proceeds of a performance of Othello to the reparation of the then existing monument. The amount was twelve pounds ten shillings. The affair dragged on, one of the Church-wardens, a blacksmith, held the £12, 10s., and was troublesome. The document of November 20, 1748, was drawn up to be signed, but was not signed, by the persons who appear to be chiefly concerned in the matter. It directed that Mr. Hall, a local limner or painter, is to "take care, according to his ability, that the monument shall become as like as possible to what it was when first erected." This appears to have been the idea of Mr.

---

[130] National Review, June 1912, p. 903.
[131] Pall Mall Gazette, November 1910.
[132] Outlines, vol. i. p. 283.

Greene. Another form of words was later adopted, directing Mr. Hall, the painter, "to repair and beautify, or to have the direction of repairing and beautifying, the original monument of Shakespeare the poet." Mrs. Stopes infers, justly in my opinion, that Hall "would fill up the gaps, restore what was amissing as he thought it ought to be, and finally repaint it according to the original colours, traces of which he might still be able to see." In his History and Antiquities of Stratford-on-Avon,[133] Mr. Wheler tells us that this was what Hall did. "In the year 1748 the monument was carefully repaired, and the original colours of the bust, &c., as much as possible preserved by Mr. John Hall, limner, of Stratford."

It follows that we see the original monument and bust, but the painting is of 1861, for the bust, says Wheler, was in 1793 "painted in white," to please Malone. It was repainted in 1861.

Mrs. Stopes, unluckily, is not content with what Hall was told to do, and what, according to Wheler, he did. She writes: "It would only be giving good value for his money" (£12, 10s.) "to his churchwardens if Hall added (sic) a cloak, a pen, and manuscript." He "could not help changing" the face, and so on.

Now it was physically impossible to add a cloak, a pen, and manuscript to such a stone bust as Dugdale's man shows; to take away the cushion pressed to the stomach, and to alter the head. Mr. Hall, if he was to give us the present bust, had to make an entirely new bust, and, to give us the present monument in place of that shown in Dugdale's print, had to construct an entirely new monument. Now Hall was a painter, not (like Giulio Romano) also an architect and sculptor. Pour tout potage he had but £12, 10s. He could not do, and he did not do these things! he did not destroy "the original monument" and make a new monument in Jacobean style. He was straitly ordered to "repair and beautify the original monument"; he did repair it, and repainted the colours. That is all. I do not quote what Halliwell-Phillipps tells us[134] about the repairing of the forefinger and thumb of the right hand, and the pen; work which, he says, had to be renewed by William Roberts of Oxford in 1790. He gives no authority, and Baconians may say that he was hoaxed, or "lied with circumstance."

Mr. Greenwood[135] quotes Halliwell-Phillipps's Works of Shakespeare (1853), in which he says that the design in Dugdale's book "is evidently too inaccurate to be of any authority; the probability being that it was not taken from the monument itself."

---

[133] P. 73, 1806.
[134] Outlines, vol. i. p. 283.
[135] The Shakespeare Problem Restated, p. 247.

Indeed the designer is so inaccurate that he gives the first word of the Latin inscription as "Judicyo," just as Oudry blunders in the Latin inscription of a portrait of Mary Stuart which he copied badly. Mr. Greenwood proceeds: "In his Outlines Halliwell simply ignores Dugdale. His engraving was doubtless too inconvenient to be brought to public notice!" Here Halliwell is accused of suppressing the truth; if he invented his minute details about the repeated reparation of the writing hand,—not represented in Dugdale's design,—he also lied with circumstance. But he certainly quoted a genuine "contemporary account" of the orders for repairing and beautifying the original monument in 1748, and I presume that he also had records for what he says about reparations of the hand and pen. He speaks, too, of substitutions for decayed alabaster parts of the monument, though not in his Outlines; and I observe that, in Mrs. Stopes's papers, there is record of a meeting on December 20, 1748, at which mention was made of "the materials" which Hall was to use for repairs.

To me the evidence of the style as to the date of both monument and bust speaks so loudly for their accepted date (1616–23) and against the Georgian date of 1748, that I need no other evidence; nor do I suppose that any one familiar with the monumental style of 1590–1620 can be of a different opinion. In the same way I do not expect any artist or engraver to take the engraving of the monument in Rowe's Shakespeare (1709), and that by Grignion so late as 1786, for anything but copies of the design in Dugdale, with modifications made à plaisir. In Pope's edition (1725) Vertue gives the monument with some approach to accuracy, but for the bald plump face of the bust presents a top-heavy and sculpturally impossible face borrowed from "the Chandos portrait," which, in my opinion, is of no more authority than any other portrait of Shakespeare. None of them, I conceive, was painted from the life.

The Baconians show a wistful longing to suppose the original bust, copied in Dugdale, to have been meant for Bacon; but we need not waste words over this speculation. Mr. Greenwood writes that "if I should be told that Dugdale's effigy represented an elderly farmer deploring an exceptionally bad harvest, 'I should not feel it to be strange!' Neither should I feel it at all strange if I were told that it was the presentment of a philosopher and Lord Chancellor, who had fallen from high estate and recognised that all things are but vanity."

"I should not feel it to be strange" if a Baconian told me that the effigy of a living ex-Chancellor were placed in the monument of the dead Will Shakspere, and if, on asking why the alteration was made, I were asked in reply, in Mr. Greenwood's words, "Was Dugdale's bust thought to bear too much resemblance to one who was not Shakspere of Stratford? Or was it thought that the presence of a woolsack" (the cushion) "might be taken as indicating that Shakspere of Stratford was indebted for support to a certain Lord Chancellor?"[136] Such, indeed, are the things that Baconians might readily say: do say, I believe.

Dugdale's engraving reproduces the first words of a Latin inscription, still on the monument:

> Judicio Pylium, genio Socratem, arte Maronem
> Terra tegit, populus mæret, Olympus habet:

"Earth covers, Olympus" (heaven? or the Muses' Hill?) "holds him who was a Nestor in counsel; in poetic art, a Virgil; a Socrates for his Dæmon" ("Genius"). As for the "Genius," or dæmon of Socrates, and the permitted false quantity in making the first syllable of Socrates short; and the use of Olympus for heaven in epitaphs, it is sufficient to consult the learning of Mr. Elton.[137] The poet who made such notable false quantities in his plays had no cause to object to another on his monument. We do not know who erected the monument, and paid for it, or who wrote or adapted the epitaph; but it was somebody who thought Shakespeare (or Bacon?) "a clayver man." The monument (if a trembling conjecture may be humbly put forth) was conceivably erected by the piety of Shakespeare's daughter and son-in-law, Mr. and Mrs. Hall. They exhibit a taste for the mortuary memorial and the queer Latin inscription. Mrs. Hall gratified the Manes of her poor mother, Mrs. Shakespeare, with one of the oddest of Latin epitaphs.[138] It opens like an epigram in the Greek Anthology, and ends in an unusual strain of Christian mysticism. Mr. Hall possesses, perhaps arranged for himself, a few Latin elegiacs as an epitaph.

The famous "Good friend for Jesus' sake forbear," and so on, on the stone in the chancel, beneath which the sacred dust of Shakespeare lies, or lay, is the first of "the last lines written, we are told,"[139] "by the author of Hamlet." Who tells us that Shakespeare wrote the four lines of doggerel? Is it conceivable that the authority for Shakespeare's authorship of the doggerel is a tradition gleaned by Mr. Dowdall of Queen's in 1693, from a parish clerk, aged over

---

[136] The Shakespeare Problem Restated, pp. 248–249.
[137] C. I. Elton, William Shakespeare, His Family and Friends, pp. 236–237.
[138] C. I. Elton, William Shakespeare, His Family and Friends, p. 228.
[139] The Shakespeare Problem Restated, p. 199.

eighty, he says,—criticism makes the clerk twenty years younger.[140] For Baconians the lines are bad enough to be the work of William Shakspere of Stratford.

Meanwhile, in 1649, when Will's daughter, Mrs. Hall, died, her epitaph spoke quite respectfully of her father's intelligence.

> "Witty above her sex, but that's not all,
> Wise to salvation was good Mistris Hall,
> Something of Shakespeare was in that, but this
> Wholly of Him with whom she's now in bliss."[141]

Thirty-three years after Shakespeare's death he was still thought "witty" in Stratford. But what could Stratford know? Milton and Charles I were of the same opinion; so was Suckling, and the rest of the generation after Shakespeare. But they did not know, how should they, that Bacon (or his equivalent) was the genuine author of the plays and poems. The secret, perhaps, so widely spread among "the friends of the Muses" in 1616, was singularly well kept by a set of men rather given to blab as a general rule.

I confess to be passing weary of the Baconian hatred of Will, which pursues him beyond his death with sneers and fantastic suspicions about his monument and his grave, and asks if he "died with a curse upon his lips, an imprecation against any man who might move his bones? A mean and vulgar curse indeed!"[142] And the authority for the circumstance that he died with a mean and vulgar curse upon his lips?

About 1694, a year after Mr. Dowdall in 1693, and eighty years almost after Shakespeare's death, W. Hall, a Queen's man, Oxford (the W. Hall, perhaps, who gave the Bodleian Aldine Ovid, with Shakespeare's signature, true or forged, to its unknown owner), went to Stratford, and wrote about his pilgrimage to his friend Mr. Thwaites, a Fellow of Queen's. Mr. Hall heard the story that Shakespeare was the author of the mean and vulgar curse. He adds that there was a great ossuary or bone-house in the church, where all the bones dug up were piled, "they would load a great number of waggons." Not desiring this promiscuity, Shakespeare wrote the Curse in a style intelligible to clerks and sextons, "for the most part a very ignorant sort of people."

If Shakespeare did, that accommodation of himself to his

---

[140] C. I. Elton, William Shakespeare, His Family and Friends, pp. 332–333.
[141] Ibid., p. 250.
[142] The Shakespeare Problem Restated, p. 199, note 1.

audience was the last stroke of his wisdom, or his wit.[143] Of course there is no evidence that he wrote the mean and vulgar curse: that he did is only the pious hope of the Baconians and Anti-Willians.

Into the question of the alleged portraits of Shakespeare I cannot enter. Ben spoke well of the engraving prefixed to the First Folio, but Ben, as Mr. Greenwood says, was anxious to give the Folio "a good send-off." The engraving is choicely bad; we do not know from what actual portrait, if from any, it was executed. Richard Burbage is known to have amused himself with the art of design; possibly he tried his hand on a likeness of his old friend and fellow-actor. If so, he may have succeeded no better than Mary Stuart's embroiderer, Oudry, in his copy of the portrait of her Majesty.

That Ben Jonson was painted by Honthorst and others, while Shakespeare, as far as we know, was not, has nothing to do with the authorship of the plays. Ben was a scholar, the darling of both Universities; constantly employed about the Court in arranging Masques; his learning and his Scottish blood may have led James I to notice him. Ben, in his later years, was much in society; fashionable and literary. He was the father of the literary "tribe of Ben." Thus he naturally sat for his portrait. In the same way George Buchanan has, and had, nothing like the fame of Knox. But as a scholar he was of European reputation; haunted the Court as tutor of his King, and was the "good pen" of the anti-Marian nobles, Murray, Morton, and the rest. Therefore Buchanan's portrait was painted, while of Knox we have only a woodcut, done, apparently, after his death, from descriptions, for Beza's Icones. The Folio engraving may have no better source. Without much minute research it is hard to find authentic portraits of Mary Stuart, and, just as in Shakespeare's case,[144] the market, in her own day and in the eighteenth century, was flooded with "mock-originals," not even derived (in any case known to me) from genuine and authentic contemporary works.

One thing is certain about the Stratford bust. Baconians will believe that Dugdale's man correctly represented the bust as it was in his time; and that the actual bust is of 1748, in spite of proofs of Dugdale's man's fantastic inaccuracy; in spite of the evidence of style; and in spite of documentary evidence that "the original monument" was not to be destroyed and replaced by the actual monument, but was merely "repaired and beautified" (painted afresh) by a local painter.

---

[143] C. I. Elton, William Shakespeare, His Family and Friends, pp. 339, 342.
[144] The Shakespeare Problem Restated, p. 238.

X

"THE TRADITIONAL SHAKSPERE"

In perusing the copious arguments of the Anti-Shakesperean but Non-Baconian Mr. Greenwood, I am often tempted, in Socratic phrase, to address him thus: Best of men, let me implore you, first, to keep in memory these statements on which you have most eloquently and abundantly insisted, namely, that society in Stratford was not only not literary, but was illiterate. Next pardon me for asking you to remember that the late sixteenth and the early seventeenth century did not resemble our fortunate age. Some people read Shakespeare's, Beaumont's, and Fletcher's plays. This exercise is now very rarely practised. But nobody cared to chronicle literary gossip about the private lives and personal traits of these and several other Elizabethan and Jacobean playwrights, in the modern manner. Of Shakespeare (pardon, I mean Shakspere), the actor, there is one contemporary anecdote, in my poor opinion a baseless waggery. Of Beaumont there is none. Of a hand-maid of Fletcher, who drank sack in a tumbler, one anecdote appears at the end of the seventeenth century,—nothing better. Meanwhile of Shakspere the "traditions" must be sought either at Stratford or in connection with the London Stage; and in both cases the traditions began to be in demand very late.

As Stratford was not literary, indeed was terribly illiterate, any traditions that survived cannot conceivably have been literary. That is absolutely certain. Natives at Stratford had, by your own hypothesis, scant interest in literary anecdote. Fifty years after Shakespeare's death, no native was likely to cherish tales of any sprouts of wit (though it was remembered in 1649, that he was "witty"), or any "wood-notes wild," which he may have displayed or chirped at an early age.

Such things were of no interest to Stratford. If he made a speech when he killed a calf, or poached, or ran away to town, the circumstance might descend from one gaffer to another; he might even be remembered as "the best of his family,"—the least inefficient. Given your non-literary and illiterate Stratford, and you can expect nothing more, and nothing better, than we receive.

Let me illustrate by a modern example. In 1866 I was an undergraduate of a year's standing at Balliol College, Oxford, certainly not an unlettered academy. In that year, the early and the best poems of a considerable Balliol poet were published: he had "gone down" some eight years before. Being young and green I eagerly sought for traditions about Mr. Swinburne. One of his contemporaries, who took a First in the final Classical Schools, told me that "he was a smug." Another, that, as Mr. Swinburne and his friend (later a Scotch professor) were not cricketers, they proposed that they should combine to pay but a single subscription to the Cricket Club. A third, a tutor of the highest reputation as a moralist and metaphysician, merely smiled at my early enthusiasm,—and told me nothing. A white-haired College servant said that "Mr. Swinburne was a very quiet gentleman."

Then you take us to dirty illiterate Stratford, from fifty to eighty years after Shakspere's death,—a Civil War and the Reign of the Saints, a Restoration and a Revolution having intervened,—and ask us to be surprised that no anecdotes of Shakspere's early brilliance, a century before, survived at Stratford.

A very humble parallel may follow. Some foolish person went seeking early anecdotes of myself at my native town, Selkirk on the Ettrick. From an intelligent townsman he gathered much that was true and interesting about my younger brothers, who delighted in horses and dogs, hunted, shot, and fished, and played cricket; one of them bowled for Gloucestershire and Oxford. But about me the inquiring literary snipe only heard that "Andra was aye the stupid ane o' the fam'ly." Yet, I, too, had bowled for the local club, non sine gloria! Even that was forgotten.

Try to remember, best of men, that literary anecdotes of a fellow townsman's youth do not dwell in the memories of his neighbours from sixty to a hundred years after date. It is not in human nature that what was incomprehensible to the grandsire should be remembered by the grandson. Go to "Thrums" and ask for literary memories of the youth of Mr. Barrie.

Yet[145] the learned Malone seems to have been sorry that little of Shakespeare but the calf-killing and the poaching, and the dying of a fever after drink taken (where, I ask you?), with Ben and Drayton, was remembered, so long after date, at Stratford, of all dirty ignorant places. Bah! how could these people have heard of Drayton and Ben? Remember that we are dealing with human nature, in a peculiarly malodorous and densely ignorant bourgade, where, however, the "wit" of Shakespeare was not forgotten (in the family) in 1649. See the epithet on the tomb of his daughter, Mrs. Hall.

You give us the Rev. John Ward, vicar of Stratford (1661–3), who has heard that the actor was "a natural wit," and contracted

---

[145] The Shakespeare Problem Restated, p. 214.

and died of a fever, after a bout with Drayton and Ben. I can scarcely believe that these were local traditions. How could these rustauds have an opinion about "natural wit," how could they have known the names of Ben and Drayton?

When you come to Aubrey, publishing in 1680, sixty years after Shakespeare's death, you neglect to trace the steps in the descent of his tradition. As has been stated, Beeston, "the chronicle of the Stage" (died 1682), gave him the story of the school-mastering; Beeston being the son of a servitor of Phillips, an actor and friend of Shakespeare, who died eleven years before that player. The story of the school-mastering and of Shakespeare "knowing Latin pretty well," is of no value to me. I think that he had some knowledge of Latin, as he must have had, if he were what I fancy him to have been, and if (which is mere hypothesis) he went for four years to a Latin School. But the story does not suit you, and you call it "a mere myth," which, "of course, will be believed by those who wish to believe it." But, most excellent of mortals, will it not, by parity of reasoning, "of course be disbelieved by those who do not wish to believe it"?

And do you want to believe it?

To several stage anecdotes of the actor as an excellent instructor of younger players, you refer slightingly. They do not weigh with me: still, the Stage would remember Shakspere (or Shakespeare) best in stage affairs. In reference to a very elliptic statement that, "in Hamlet Betterton benefited by Shakespeare's coaching," you write, "This is astonishing, seeing that Shakspere had been in his grave nearly twenty years when Betterton was born. The explanation is that Taylor, of the Black Fryars Company, was, according to Sir William Davenant, instructed by Shakspere, and Davenant, who had seen Taylor act, according to Downes, instructed Betterton. There is a similar story about Betterton playing King Henry VIII. Betterton was said to have been instructed by Sir William, who was instructed by Lowen, who was instructed by Shakspere!"[146]

Why a note of exclamation? Who was Downes, and what were his opportunities of acquiring information? He "was for many years book-keeper in the Duke's Company, first under Davenant in the old house..." Davenant was notoriously the main link between "the first and second Temple," the theatre of Shakespeare whom, as a boy, he knew, and the Restoration theatre. Devoted to the traditions of the stage, he collected Shakespearean and other anecdotes; he revived the theatre, cautiously, during the last years of Puritan rule, and

---

[146] The Shakespeare Problem Restated, p. 214, note 2.

told his stories to the players of the early Restoration. As his Bookkeeper with the Duke of York's Company, Downes heard what Davenant had to tell; he also, for his Roscius Anglicanus, had notes from Charles Booth, prompter at Drury Lane. On May 28, 1663, Davenant reproduced Hamlet, with young Betterton as the Prince of Denmark. Davenant, says Charles Booth, "had seen the part taken by Taylor, of the Black Fryars Company, and Taylor had been instructed by the author," (not Bacon but) "Mr. William Shakespeare," and Davenant "taught Mr. Betterton in every particle of it." Mr. Elton adds, "We cannot be sure that Taylor was taught by Shakespeare himself. He is believed to have been a member of the King's Company before 1613, and to have left it for a time before Shakespeare's death."[147] His name is in the list in the Folio of "the principall Actors in all these plays," but I cannot pretend to be certain that he played in them in Will's time.

It is Mr. Pepys (December 30, 1668) who chronicles Davenant's splendid revival of Henry VIII, in which Betterton, as the King, was instructed by Sir William Davenant, who had it from old Mr. Lowen, that had his instruction "from Mr. Shakespear himself." Lowin, or Lowen, joined Shakespeare's Company in 1604, being then a man of twenty-eight. Burbage was the natural man for Hamlet and Henry VIII; but it is not unusual for actors to have "understudies."

The stage is notoriously tenacious of such traditions.

When we come with you to Mr. W. Fulman, about 1688, and the additions to his notes made about 1690–1708, we are concerned with evidence much too remote, and, in your own classical style, "all this is just a little mixed."[148] With what Mr. Dowdall heard in 1693, and Mr. William Hall (1694) heard from a clerk or sexton, or other illiterate dotard at Stratford, I have already dealt. I do not habitually believe in what I hear from "the oldest aunt telling the saddest tale,"—no, not even if she tells a ghost story, or an anecdote about the presentation by Queen Mary of her portrait to the ancestor of the Laird,—the portrait being dated 1768, and representing her Majesty in the bloom of girlhood. Nor do I care for what Rowe said (on Betterton's information), in 1709, about Shakespeare's schooling; nor for what Dr. Furnivall said that Plume wrote; nor for what anybody said that Sir John Mennes (Menzies?) said. But I do care for what Ben Jonson and Shakespeare's fellow-actors said; and for what his literary contemporaries have left on record. But this evidence you explain away by ætiological guesses, absolutely

---

[147] C. I. Elton, William Shakespeare, His Family and Friends, p. 56.
[148] The Shakespeare Problem Restated, pp. 28, 29.

modern, and, I conceive, to anyone familiar with historical inquiry, not more valuable as history than other explanatory myths.

What Will Shakspere had to his literary credit when he died, was men's impressions of the seeing of his acted plays; with their knowledge, if they had any, of fugitive, cheap, perishable, and often bad reprints, in quartos, of about half of the plays. Men also had Venus and Adonis, Lucrece, and the Sonnets, which sold very poorly, and I do not wonder at it. Of the genius of Shakespeare England could form no conception, till the publication of the Folio (1623), not in a large edition; it struggled into a Third Edition in 1664. The engouement about the poet, the search for personal details, did not manifest itself with any vigour till nearly thirty years after 1664—and we are to wonder that the gleanings, at illiterate Stratford, and in Stage tradition, are so scanty and so valueless. What could have been picked up, by 1680–90, about Bacon at Gorhambury, or in the Courts of Law, I wonder.

XI

THE FIRST FOLIO

"The First Folio" is the name commonly given to the first collected edition of Shakespeare's plays. The volume includes a Preface signed by two of the actors, Heminge and Condell, panegyrical verses by Ben Jonson and others, and a bad engraved portrait. The book has been microscopically examined by Baconians, hunting for cyphered messages from their idol in italics, capital letters, misprints, and everywhere. Their various discoveries do not win the assent of writers like the late Lord Penzance and Mr. Greenwood.

The mystery as to the sources, editing, and selection of plays in the Folio (1623) appears to be impenetrable. The title-page says that all the contents are published "according to the true original copies." If only MS. copies are meant, this is untrue; in some cases the best quartos were the chief source, supplemented by MSS. The Baconians, following Malone, think that Ben Jonson wrote the Preface (and certainly it looks like his work),[149] speaking in the name of the two actors who sign it. They say that Shakespeare's friends "have collected and published" the plays, have so published them "that whereas you were abus'd with divers stolne and surreptitious copies, maimed and deformed by the frauds and stealthes of injurious impostors that exposed them: even those" (namely, the pieces previously ill-produced by pirates) "are now offered to your view cur'd, and perfect of their limbes; and all the rest" (that is, all the plays which had not been piratically debased), "absolute in their numbers, as he conceived them." So obscure is the Preface that not all previously published separate plays are explicitly said to be stolen and deformed, but "divers stolen copies" are denounced. Mr. Pollard makes the same point in Shakespeare Folios and Quartos, p. 2 (1909).

Now, as a matter of fact, while some of the quarto editions of separate plays are very bad texts, others are so good that the Folio sometimes practically reprints them, with some tinkerings, from manuscripts. Some quartos, like that of Hamlet of 1604, are excellent, and how they came to be printed from good texts, and whether or not the texts were given to the press by Shakespeare's Company, or were sold, or stolen, is the question. Mr. Pollard

---

[149] Like Mr. Greenwood, I think that Ben was the penman.

argues, on grounds almost certain, that "we have strong prima facie evidence that the sale to publishers of plays afterwards duly entered on the Stationers' Registers was regulated by their lawful owners."[150]

The Preface does not explicitly deny that some of the separately printed texts were good, but says that "divers" of them were stolen and deformed. My view of the meaning of the Preface is not generally held. Dr. H. H. Furness, in his preface to Much Ado about Nothing (p. vi), says, "We all know that these two friends of Shakespeare assert in their Preface to the Folio that they had used the Author's manuscripts, and in the same breath denounce the Quartos as stolen and surreptitious." I cannot see, I repeat, that the Preface denounces all the Quartos. It could be truly said that divers stolen and maimed copies had been foisted on "abused" purchasers, and really no more is said. Dr. Furness writes, "When we now find them using as 'copy' one of these very Quartos" (Much Ado about Nothing, 1600), "we need not impute to them a wilful falsehood if we suppose that in using what they knew had been printed from the original text, howsoever obtained, they held it to be the same as the manuscript itself..." That was their meaning, I think, the Quarto of Much Ado had not been "maimed" and "deformed," as divers other quartos, stolen and surreptitious, had been.

Shakspere, unlike most of the other playwrights, was a member of his Company. I presume that his play was thus the common good of his Company and himself. If they sold a copy to the press, the price would go into their common stock; unless they, in good will, allowed the author to pocket the money.

It will be observed that I understand the words of the Preface otherwise than do the distinguished Editors of the Cambridge edition. They write, "The natural inference to be drawn from this statement" (in the Preface) "is that all the separate editions of Shakespeare's plays were 'stolen,' 'surreptitious' and imperfect, and that all those published in the Folio were printed from the author's own manuscripts" (my italics). The Editors agree with Dr. Furness, not with Mr. Pollard, whose learned opinion coincides with my own.

Perhaps it should be said that I reached my own construction of the sense of this passage in the Preface by the light of nature, before Mr. Pollard's valuable book, based on the widest and most minute research, came into my hands. By the results of that research he backs his opinion (and mine), that some of the quartos are surreptitious and bad, while others are good "and were honestly

---

[150] Pollard, ut supra, p. 10.

obtained."[151] The Preface never denies this; never says that all the quartos contain maimed and disfigured texts. The Preface draws a distinction to this effect, "even those" (even the stolen and deformed copies) "are now cured and perfect in their limbs,"—that is, have been carefully edited, while "all the rest" are "absolute in their numbers as he conceived them." This does not allege that all the rest are printed from Shakespeare's own holograph copies.

Among the plays spoken of as "all the rest," namely, those not hitherto published and not deformed by the fraudulent, are, Tempest, Two Gentlemen, Measure for Measure, Comedy of Errors, As You Like It, All's Well, Twelfth Night, Winter's Tale, Henry VI, iii., Henry VIII, Coriolanus, Timon, Julius Cæsar, Macbeth, Antony and Cleopatra, and Cymbeline. Also Henry VI, i., ii., King John, and Taming of the Shrew, appeared now in other form than in the hitherto published Quartos bearing these or closely similar names. We have, moreover, no previous information as to The Shrew, Timon, Julius Cæsar, All's Well, and Henry VIII. The Preface adds the remarkable statement that, whatever Shakespeare thought, "he uttered with that easinesse, that wee have scarce received from him a blot in his papers."

It is plain that the many dramas previously unpublished could only be recovered from manuscripts of one sort or another, because they existed in no other form. The Preface takes it for granted that the selected manuscripts contain the plays "absolute in their numbers as he conceived them." But the Preface does not commit itself, I repeat, to the statement that all of these many plays are printed from Shakespeare's own handwriting. After "as he conceived them," it goes on, "Who, as he was a most happy imitator of nature, was a most gentle expresser of it. His mind and hand went together: and what he thought he uttered with that easiness, that we have scarce received from him a blot in his papers."

This may be meant to suggest, but does not affirm, that the actors have "all the rest" of the plays in Shakespeare's own handwriting. They may have, or may have had, some of his manuscripts, and believed that other manuscripts accessible to them, and used by them, contain his very words. Whether from cunning or design, or from the Elizabethan inability to tell a plain tale plainly, the authors or author of the Preface have everywhere left themselves loopholes and ways of evasion and escape. It is not possible to pin them down to any plain statement of facts concerning the sources for the hitherto unpublished plays, "the rest" of the plays.

---

[151] Pollard, ut supra, pp. 64–80.

These, at least, were from manuscript sources which the actors thought accurate, and some may have been "fair copies" in Shakespeare's own hand. (Scott, as regards his novels, sent his prima cura, his first writing down, to the press, and his pages are nearly free from blot or erasion. In one case at least, Shelley's first draft of a poem is described as like a marsh of reeds in water, with wild ducks, but he made very elegant fair copies for the press.) Let it be supposed that Ben Jonson wrote all this Preface, in accordance with the wishes and instructions of the two actors who sign it. He took their word for the almost blotless MSS. which they received from Shakespeare. He remarks, in his posthumously published Discoveries (notes, memories, brief essays), "I remember the players have often mentioned it as an honour to Shakespeare, that in his writing (whatsoever he penned) he never blotted out a line." And Ben gives, we shall later see, his habitual reply to this habitual boast.

As to the sources of such plays as had been "maimed and deformed by injurious impostors," and are now "offered cur'd and perfect of their limbs," "it can be proved to demonstration," say the Cambridge Editors, "that several plays in the Folio were printed from earlier quarto editions" (but the players secured a retreat on this point), "and that in other cases the quarto is more correctly printed, or from a better manuscript than the Folio text, and therefore of higher authority." Hamlet, in the Folio of 1623, when it differs from the quarto of 1604, "differs for the worse in forty-seven places, while it differs for the better in twenty places."

Can the wit of man suggest any other explanation than that the editing of the Folio was carelessly done; out of the best quartos and MSS. in the theatre for acting purposes, and,—if the players did not lie in what they "often said," and if they kept the originals,—out of some MSS. received from Shakspere? Whether the two players themselves threw into the press, after some hasty botchings, whatever materials they had, or whether they employed an Editor, a very wretched Editor, or Editors, or whether the great Author, Bacon, himself was his own Editor, the preparation of a text was infamously done. The two actors, probably, I think, never read through the proof-sheets, and took the word of the man whom they employed to edit their materials, for gospel. The editing of the Folio is so exquisitely careless that twelve printer's errors in a quarto of 1622, of Richard III, appear in the Folio of 1623. Again, the Merry Wives of the Folio, is nearly twice as long as the quarto of 1619, yet keeps old errors.

How can we explain the reckless retention of errors, and also the large additions and improvements? Did the true author (Bacon or Bungay) now edit his work, add much matter, and go wrong forty-seven times where the quarto was right, and go right twenty times when the quarto was wrong? Did he, for the Folio of 1623, nearly double The Merry Wives in extent, and also leave all the errors of the fourth quarto uncorrected?

In that case how negligent was Bacon of his immortal works! Now Bacon was a scholar, and this absurd conduct cannot be imputed, I hope, to him.

Mr. Pollard is much more lenient than his fellow-scholars towards the Editor or Editors of the Folio. He concludes that "manuscript copies of the plays were easily procurable." Sixteen out of the thirty-six plays existed in quartos. Eight of the sixteen were not used for the Folio; five were used, "with additions, corrections, or alterations" (which must have been made from manuscripts). Three quartos only were reprinted as they stood. The Editors greatly preferred to use manuscript copies; and showed this, Mr. Pollard thinks, by placing plays, never before printed, in the most salient parts of the three sets of dramas in their book.[152] They did make an attempt to divide their plays into Acts and Scenes, whereas the quartos, as a general rule, had been undivided. But the Editors, I must say, had not the energy to carry out their good intentions fully—or Bacon or Bungay, if the author, wearied in well-doing. The work is least ill done in the Comedies, and grows worse and worse as the Editor, or Bacon, or Bungay becomes intolerably slack.

A great living author, who had a decent regard for his own works, could never have made or passed this slovenly Folio. Yet Mr. Greenwood argues that probably Bungay was still alive and active, after Shakspere was dead and buried. (Mr. Greenwood, of course, does not speak of Bungay, which I use as short for his Great Unknown.) Thus, Richard III from 1597 to 1622 appeared in six quartos. It is immensely improved in the Folio, and so are several other plays. Who made the improvements, which the Editors could only obtain in manuscripts? If we say that Shakespeare made them in MS., Mr. Greenwood asks, "What had he to work upon, since, after selling his plays to his company, he did not preserve his manuscript?"[153] Now I do not know that he did sell his plays to his company. We are sure that Will got money for them, but we do not know what arrangement he made with his company. He may have had an author's rights in addition to a sum down, as later was customary, and he had his regular share in the profits. Nor am I possessed of information that "he did not preserve his manuscript."

---

[152] Pollard, ut supra, pp. 121–124.
[153] The Shakespeare Problem Restated, pp. 287–288.

How can we know that? He may have kept his first draft, he may have made a fair copy for himself, as well as for the players, or may have had one made. He may have worked on a copy possessed by the players; and the publisher of the quartos of 1605, 1612, 1622, may not have been allowed to use, or may not have asked for the latest manuscript revised copy. The Richard III of the Folio contains, with much new matter, the printer's errors of the quarto of 1622. I would account for this by supposing that the casual Editor had just sense enough to add the new parts in a revised manuscript to the quarto, and was far too lazy to correct the printer's errors in the quarto. But Mr. Greenwood asks whether "the natural conclusion is not that 'some person unknown' took the Quarto of 1622, revised it, added the new passages, and thus put it into the form in which it appeared in 1623." This natural conclusion means that the author, Bungay, was alive in 1622, and put his additions and improvements of recent date into the quarto of 1622, but never took the trouble to correct the errors in the quarto. And so on in other plays similarly treated. "Is it not a more natural conclusion that 'Shakespeare'" (Bungay) "himself revised its publication, and that some part of this revision, at any rate, was done after 1616 and before 1623."[154]

Mr. Greenwood, after criticising other systems, writes,[155] "There is, of course, another hypothesis. It is that Shakespeare" (meaning the real author) "did not die in 1616," and here follows the usual notion that "Shakespeare" was the "nom de plume" of that transcendent genius, "moving in Court circles among the highest of his day (as assuredly Shakespeare must have moved)—who wished to conceal his identity."

I have not the shadow of assurance that the Author "moved in Court circles," though Will would see a good deal when he played at Court, and in the houses of nobles, before "Eliza and our James." I never moved in Court circles: Mr. Greenwood must know them better than I do, and I have explained (see Love's Labour's Lost, and Shakespeare, Genius, and Society) how Will picked up his notions of courtly ways.

"Another hypothesis," the Baconian hypothesis,—"nom de plume" and all,—Mr. Greenwood thinks "an extremely reasonable one": I cannot easily conceive of one more unreasonable.

"Supposing that there was such an author as I have suggested, he may well have conceived the idea of publishing a collected edition of the plays which had been written under the name of

---

[154] The Shakespeare Problem Restated, pp. 290–291.
[155] Ibid., pp. 292, 293.

Shakespeare, and being himself busy with other matters, he may have entrusted the business to some 'literary man,' to some 'good pen,' who was at the time doing work for him; and why not to the man who wrote the commendatory verses, the 'Lines to the Reader'" (opposite to the engraving), "and, as seems certain, the Preface, 'to the great variety of Readers'?"[156]

That man, that "good pen," was Ben Jonson. On the "supposing" of Mr. Greenwood, Ben is "doing work for" the Great Unknown at the time when "the business" following on the "idea of publishing a collected edition of the plays which had been written under the name of Shakespeare" occurred to the illustrious but unknown owner of that "nom de plume." In plain words of my own,—the Author may have entrusted "the business," and what was that business if not the editing of the Folio?—to Ben Jonson—"who was at the time doing work for him"—for the Author.

Here is a clue! We only need to know for what man of "transcendent genius, universal culture, world-wide philosophy ... moving in Court circles," and so on, Ben "was working" about 1621–3, the Folio appearing in 1623.

The heart beats with anticipation of a discovery! "On January 22, 1621, Bacon celebrated his sixtieth birthday with great state at York House. Jonson was present," and wrote an ode, with something about the Genius of the House (Lar or Brownie),

"Thou stand'st as if some mystery thou didst."

Mr. Greenwood does not know what this can mean; nor do I.[157]

"Jonson, it appears" (on what authority?), "was Bacon's guest at Gorhambury, and was one of those good 'pens,'" of whom Bacon speaks as assisting him in the translation of some of his books into Latin.

Bacon, writing to Toby Mathew, June 26, 1623, mentions the help of "some good pens," Ben Jonson he does not mention. But Judge Webb does. "It is an undoubted fact," says Judge Webb, "that the Latin of the De Augmentis, which was published in 1623, was the work of Jonson."[158] To whom Mr. Collins replies, "There is not a particle of evidence that Jonson gave to Bacon the smallest assistance in translating any of his works into Latin."[159]

Très bien, on Judge Webb's assurance the person for whom

---

[156] The Shakespeare Problem Restated, p. 293.
[157] The Shakespeare Problem Restated, pp. 489, 490.
[158] Ibid., p. 491.
[159] Studies in Shakespeare, p. 352.

Ben was working, in 1623, was Bacon. Meanwhile, Mr. Greenwood's "supposing" is "that there was such an author" (of transcendent genius, and so on), who "may have entrusted the editing of his collected plays" to some "good pen," who was at the time "doing work for him," and "why not to"—Ben Jonson.[160] Now the man for whom Ben, in 1623, was "doing work"—was Bacon,—so Judge Webb says.[161]

Therefore, by this hypothesis of Mr. Greenwood,[162] the Great Unknown was Bacon,—just the hypothesis of the common Baconian.

Is my reasoning erroneous? Is the "supposing" suggested by Mr. Greenwood[163] any other than that of Miss Delia Bacon, and Judge Webb? True, Mr. Greenwood's Baconian "supposing" is only a working hypothesis: not a confirmed belief. But it is useful to his argument (see "Ben Jonson and Shakespeare") when he wants to explain away Ben's evidence, in his verses in the Folio, to the Stratford actor as the Author.

Mr. Greenwood writes, in the first page of his Preface: "It is no part of my plan or intention to defend that theory," "the Baconian theory." Apparently it pops out contrary to the intention of Mr. Greenwood. But pop out it does: at least I can find no flaw in the reasoning of my detection of Bacon: I see no way out of it except this: after recapitulating what is said about Ben as one of Bacon's "good pens" with other details, Mr. Greenwood says, "But no doubt that way madness lies!"[164] Ah no! not madness, no, but Baconism "lies that way." However, "let it be granted" (as Euclid says in his sportsmanlike way) that Mr. Greenwood by no means thinks that his "concealed poet" is Bacon—only some one similar and similarly situated and still active in 1623, and occupied with other business than supervising a collected edition of plays written under his "nom de plume" of Shakespeare. Bacon, too, was busy, with supervising, or toiling at the Latin translation of his scientific works, and Ben (according to Judge Webb) was busy in turning the Advancement of Learning into Latin prose. Mr. Greenwood quotes, without reference, Archbishop Tenison as saying that Ben helped Bacon in doing his works into Latin.[165] Tenison is a very late witness. The prophetic soul of Bacon did not quite trust English to last as long as

---

[160] The Shakespeare Problem Restated, p. 293.
[161] Ibid., p. 491.
[162] Ibid., p. 293.
[163] Ibid., p. 293.
[164] The Shakespeare Problem Restated, p. 297.
[165] The Shakespeare Problem Restated, p. 297.

Latin, or he thought Latin, the lingua franca of Europe in his day, more easily accessible to foreign students, as, of course, it was. Thus Bacon was very busy; so was Ben. The sad consequence of Ben's business, perhaps, is that the editing of the Folio is notoriously bad; whether Ben were the Editor or not, it is infamously bad.

Conceivably Mr. Greenwood is of the same opinion. He says, "It stands admitted that a very large part of that volume" (the Folio) "consists of work that is not 'Shakespeare's' at all."

How strange, if Ben edited it for the Great Unknown—who knew, if any human being knew, what work was "Shakespeare's"! On Mr. Greenwood's hypothesis,[166] or "supposing," the Unknown Author "may well have conceived the idea of publishing a collected edition of the plays which had been written" (not "published," written) "under the name of Shakespeare, and, being himself busy with other matters, he may have entrusted the business to" some "good pen," "and why not to"—Ben. Nevertheless "a very large part of that volume consists of work that is not 'Shakespeare's' at all."[167] How did this occur? The book[168] is "that very doubtful 'canon.'" How, if "Shakespeare's" man edited it for "Shakespeare"? Did "Shakespeare" not care what stuff was placed under his immortal "nom de plume"?

It is not my fault if I think that Mr. Greenwood's hypotheses[169]—the genuine "Shakespeare" either revised his own works, or put Ben on the editorial task—are absolutely contradicted by his statements in another part of his book.[170] For the genuine "Shakespeare" knew what plays he had written, knew what he could honestly put forth as his own, as "Shakespeare's." Or, if he placed the task of editing in Ben's hands, he must have told Ben what plays were of his own making. In either case the Folio would contain these, and no others. But—"the plat contraire,"—the very reverse,—is stated by Mr. Greenwood. "It stands admitted that a very large portion of that volume" (the Folio) "consists of work that is not 'Shakespeare's'" (is not Bacon's, or the other man's) "at all."[171] Then away fly the hypotheses[172] that the auto-Shakespeare, or that Ben, employed by the auto-Shakespeare (apparently Bacon) revised, edited, and prepared for publication the auto-Shakespearean plays.

---

[166] The Shakespeare Problem Restated, p. 293.
[167] Ibid., p. 351.
[168] Ibid., p. 351.
[169] Ibid., pp. 290, 293.
[170] Ibid., pp. 351, 358.
[171] The Shakespeare Problem Restated, p. 351.
[172] Ibid., pp. 290, 293.

For Mr. Greenwood "has already dealt with Titus (Andronicus) and Henry VI,"[173] and proved them not to be auto-Shakespearean—and he adds "there are many other plays in that very doubtful 'canon'" (the Folio) "which, by universal admission, contain much non-Shakespearean composition."[174] Perhaps! but if so the two hypotheses,[175] that either the genuine Shakespeare[176] revised ("is it not a more natural solution that 'Shakespeare' himself revised his works for publication, and that some part, at any rate, of this revision[177] was done after 1616 and before 1623?"), or[178] that he gave Ben (who was working, by the conjecture, for Bacon) the task of editing the Folio,—are annihilated. For neither the auto-Shakespeare (if honest), nor Ben (if sober), could have stuffed the Folio full of non-Shakespearean work,—including four "non-Shakespearean" plays,—nor could the Folio be "that very doubtful canon."[179] Again, if either the auto-Shakespeare or Ben following his instructions, were Editor, neither could have, as the Folio Editor had "evidently no little doubt about" Troilus and Cressida.[180]

Neither Ben, nor the actual Simon Pure, the author, the auto-Shakespeare, could fail to know the truth about Trodus and Cressida. But the Editor[181] did not know the truth, the whole canon is "doubtful." Therefore the hypothesis, the "supposing," that the actual author did the revising,[182] and the other hypothesis that he gave Ben the work,[183] seem to me wholly impossible. But Mr. Greenwood needs the "supposings" of pp. 290, 293; and as he rejects Titus Andronicus and Henry VI (both in the Folio), he also needs the contradictory views of pp. 351, 358. On which set of supposings and averments does he stand to win?

Perhaps he thinks to find a way out of what appears to me to be a dilemma in the following fashion: He will not accept Titus Andronicus and Henry VI, though both are in the Folio, as the work of his "Shakespeare," his Unknown, the Bacon of the Baconians. Well, we ask, if your Unknown, or Bacon, or Ben,—instructed by

---

[173] Ibid., p. 351.
[174] Ibid., p. 351.
[175] Ibid., pp. 290, 293.
[176] Ibid., p. 290.
[177] Ibid., pp. 290, 291.
[178] Ibid., p. 293.
[179] The Shakespeare Problem Restated, p. 351.
[180] Ibid., p. 358.
[181] Ibid., pp. 351, 358.
[182] Ibid., p. 290.
[183] Ibid., p. 293.

Bacon, or by the Unknown,—edited the Folio, how could any one of the three insert Titus, and Henry VI, and be "in no little doubt about" Troilus and Cressida? Bacon, or the Unknown, or the Editor employed by either, knew perfectly well which plays either man could honestly claim as his own work, done under the "nom de plume" of "William Shakespeare" (with or without the hyphen). Yet the Editor of the Folio does not know—and Mr. Greenwood does know—Henry VI and Titus are "wrong ones."

Mr. Greenwood's way out, if I follow him, is this:[184] "Judge Stotsenburg asks, 'Who wrote The Taming of a Shrew printed in 1594, and who wrote Titus Andronicus, Henry VI, or King Lear referred to in the Diary?'" (Henslowe's). The Judge continues: "Neither Collier nor any of the Shaxper commentators make (sic) any claim to their authorship in behalf of William Shaxper. Since these plays have the same names as those included in the Folio of 1623 the presumption is that they are the same plays until the contrary is shown. Of course it may be shown, either that those in the Folio are entirely different except in name, or that these plays were revised, improved, and dressed by some one whom they" (who?) "called Shakespeare."

Mr. Greenwood says, "My own conviction is that ... these plays were 'revised, improved, and dressed by some one whom they called Shakespeare.'"[185] (Whom who called Shakespeare?) In that case these plays,—say Titus Andronicus and Henry VI, Part 1,—which Mr. Greenwood denies to his "Shakespeare" were just as much his Shakespeare's plays as any other plays (and there are several), which his Shakespeare "revised, improved, and dressed." Yet his Shakespeare is not author of Henry VI,[186] not the author of Titus Andronicus.[187] "Mr. Anders," writes Mr. Greenwood, "makes what I think to be a great error in citing Henry VI and Titus as genuine plays of Shakespeare."[188]

He hammers at this denial in nineteen references in his Index to Titus Andronicus. Yet Ben, or Bacon, or the Unknown thought that these plays were "genuine plays" of "Shakespeare," the concealed author—Bacon or Mr. Greenwood's man. It appears that the immense poet who used the "nom de plume" of "Shakespeare" did not know the plays of which he could rightfully call himself the author; that (not foreseeing Mr. Greenwood's constantly repeated

---

[184] The Shakespeare Problem Restated, pp. 355, 356.
[185] The Shakespeare Problem Restated, pp. 355, 356.
[186] Ibid., pp. 158, 160, 162 ("not the original author"), 170.
[187] Ibid., pp. 130–151, 160, 168.
[188] Ibid., p., 123, note 2.

objections) he boldly annexed four plays, or two certainly, which Mr. Greenwood denies to him, and another about which "the Folio Editor was in no little doubt."

Finally,[189] Mr. Greenwood is "convinced," "it is my conviction" that some plays which he often denies to his "Shakespeare" were "revised, improved, and dressed by some one whom they called Shakespeare." That some one, if he edited or caused to be edited the Folio, thought that his revision, improvement, and dressing up of the plays gave him a right to claim their authorship—and Mr. Greenwood, a dozen times and more, denies to him their authorship.

One is seriously puzzled to discover the critic's meaning. The Taming of a Shrew, Titus, Henry VI, and King Lear, referred to in Henslowe's "Diary," are not "Shakespearean," we are repeatedly told. But "my own conviction is that..." these plays were "revised, improved, and dressed by some one whom they called Shakespeare." But to be revised, improved, and dressed by some one whom they called Shakespeare, is to be as truly "Shakespearean" work as is any play so handled "by Shakespeare." Thus the plays mentioned are as truly "Shakespearean" as any others in which "Shakespeare" worked on an earlier canvas, and also Titus "is not Shakespearean at all." Mr. Greenwood, I repeat, constantly denies the "Shakespearean" character to Titus and Henry VI. "The conclusion of the whole matter is that Titus and The Trilogy of Henry VI are not the work of Shakespeare: that his hand is probably not to be found at all in Titus, and only once or twice, if at all, in Henry VI, Part I, but that he it probably was who altered and remodelled the two parts of the old Contention of the Houses of York and Lancaster, thereby producing Henry VI, Parts II and III."[190]

Yet[191] Titus and Henry VI appear as "revised, improved, and dressed" by the mysterious "some one whom they called Shakespeare." If Mr. Greenwood's conclusion[192] be correct, "Shakespeare" had no right to place Henry VI, Part I, and Titus in his Folio. If his "conviction"[193] be correct, Shakespeare had as good a right to them as to any of the plays which he revised, and improved, and dressed. They must be "Shakespearean" if Mr. Greenwood is right[194] in his suggestion that "Shakespeare" either

---

[189] The Shakespeare Problem Restated, p. 356.
[190] The Shakespeare Problem Restated, p. 160.
[191] Ibid., p. 356.
[192] Ibid., p. 160.
[193] Ibid., p. 356.
[194] Ibid., pp. 290, 293.

revised his works for publication between 1616 and 1623, or set his man, Ben Jonson, upon that business. Yet neither one nor the other knew what to make of Troilus and Cressida. "The Folio Editor had, evidently, no little doubt about that play."[195]

So neither "Shakespeare" nor Ben, instructed by him, can have been "the Folio Editor." Consequently Mr. Greenwood must abandon his suggestion that either man was the Editor, and may return to his rejection of Titus and Henry VI, Part I. But he clings to it. He finds in Henslowe's Diary "references to, and records of the writing of, such plays" as, among others, Titus Andronicus, and Henry VI.[196]

Mr. Greenwood, after rejecting a theory of some one, says, "Far more likely does it appear that there was a great man of the time whose genius was capable of 'transforming dross into gold,' who took these plays, and, in great part, rewrote and revised them, leaving sometimes more, and sometimes less of the original work; and that so rewritten, revised, and transformed they appeared as the plays of 'Shake-speare.'"[197]

This statement is made[198] about "these plays," including Titus Andronicus and Henry VI, while[199] "Titus and the Trilogy of Henry VI are not the work of Shakespeare ... his hand is probably not to be found at all in Titus, and only once or twice in Henry VI, Part I," though he probably made Parts II and III out of older plays.

I do not know where to have the critic. If Henry VI, Part I, and Titus are in no sense by "Shakespeare," then neither "Shakespeare" nor Ben for him edited or had anything to do with the editing of the Folio. If either or both had to do with the editing, as the critic suggests, then he is wrong in denying Shakespearean origin to Titus and Henry VI, Part I.

Of course one sees a way out of the dilemma for the great auto-Shakespeare himself, who, by one hypothesis, handed over the editing of his plays to Ben (he, by Mr. Greenwood's "supposing," was deviling at literary jobs for Bacon). The auto-Shakespeare merely tells Ben to edit his plays, and never even gives him a list of them. Then Ben brings him the Folio, and the author looks at the list of Plays.

---

[195] Ibid., p. 358.
[196] The Shakespeare Problem Restated, p. 365. I will bet Mr. Greenwood any sum not exceeding half a crown that he cannot find any "records of the writing of" either of these plays in Henslowe's "Diary,"—his account book of expenses and receipts.
[197] Ibid., p. 365.
[198] Ibid., p. 365.
[199] Ibid., p. 160.

"Mr. Jonson," he says, "I have hitherto held thee for an honest scholar and a deserving man in the quality thou dost profess. But thou hast brought me a maimed and deformed printed copy of that which I did write for my own recreation, not wishful to be known for so light a thing as a poet. Moreover, thou hast placed among these my trifles, four plays to which I never put a finger, and others in which I had no more than a thumb. The Seneschal, Mr. Jonson, will pay thee what is due to thee; thy fardels shall be sent whithersoever thou wilt, and, Mary! Mr. Jonson, I bid thee never more be officer of mine."

This painful discourse must have been held at Gorhambury,—if Ben edited the Folio—for Francis.

It is manifest, I hope, that about the Folio Mr. Greenwood speaks with two voices, and these very discordant. It is also manifest that, whoever wrote the plays left his materials in deep neglect, and that, when they were collected, some one gathered them up in extreme disorder. It is extraordinary that the Baconians and Mr. Greenwood do not see the fallacy of their own reasoning in this matter of the Folio. They constantly ridicule the old view that the actor, Will Shakspere (if, by miracle, he were the author of the plays), could have left them to take their fortunes. They are asked, what did other playwrights do in that age? They often parted with their whole copyright to the actors of this or that company, or to Henslowe. The new owners could alter the plays at will, and were notoriously anxious to keep them out of print, lest other companies should act them. As Mr. Greenwood writes,[200] "Such, we are told, was the universal custom with dramatists of the day; they 'kept no copies' of their plays, and thought no more about them. It will, I suppose, be set down to fanaticism that I should doubt the truth of this proposition, that I doubt if it be consonant with the known facts of human nature." But whom, except Jonson, does Mr. Greenwood find editing and publishing his plays? Beaumont, Fletcher, Heywood? No!

If the Great Unknown were dead in 1623, his negligence was as bad as Will's. If he were alive and revised his own work for publication,[201] he did it as the office cat might have done it in hours of play. If, on the other side, he handed the editorial task over to Ben,[202] then he did not even give Ben a list of his genuine works. Mr. Greenwood cites the case of Ben Jonson, a notorious and, I think, solitary exception. Ben was and often proclaimed himself to

---

[200] The Shakespeare Problem Restated, p. 276.
[201] Ibid., p. 290.
[202] The Shakespeare Problem Restated, p. 293.

be essentially a scholar. He took as much pains in prefacing, editing, and annotating his plays, as he would have taken had the texts been those of Greek tragedians.

Finally, all Baconians cry out against the sottish behaviour of the actor, Will, if being really the author of the plays, he did not bestir himself, and bring them out in a collected edition. Yet no English dramatist ventured on doing such a thing, till Ben thus collected his "works" (and was laughed at) in 1616. The example might have encouraged Will to be up and doing, but he died early in 1616. If Will were not the author, what care was Bacon, or the Unknown, taking of his many manuscript plays, and for the proper editing of those which had appeared separately in pamphlets? As indolent and casual as Will, the great Author, Bacon or another, left the plays to take their chances. Mr. Greenwood says that "if the author" (Bacon or somebody very like him) "had been careless about keeping copies of his manuscripts ... "[203] What an "if" in the case of the great Author! This gross neglect, infamous in Will, may thus have been practised by the Great Unknown himself.

In 1911 Mr. Greenwood writes, "There is overwhelming authority for the view that Titus Andronicus is not Shakespearean at all."[204] In that case, neither Bacon, nor the Unknown, nor Ben, acting for either, can have been the person who put Titus into the Folio.

---

[203] Ibid., p. 294.
[204] The Vindicators of Shakespeare, p. 57 (1911).

XII

BEN JONSON AND SHAKESPEARE

The evidence of Ben Jonson to the identity of Shakespeare the author with Shakspere the actor, is "the strength of the Stratfordian faith," says Mr. Greenwood. "But I think it will be admitted that the various Jonsonian utterances with regard to 'Shakespeare' are by no means easy to reconcile one with the other."[205]

It is difficult to reply briefly to Mr. Greenwood's forty-seven pages about the evidence of Jonson. But, first, whenever in written words or in reported conversation, Ben speaks of Shakespeare by name, he speaks of his works: in 1619 to Drummond of Hawthornden; in 1623 in commendatory verses to the Folio; while, about 1630, probably, in his posthumously published Discourses, he writes on Shakespeare as the friend and "fellow" of the players, on Shakespeare as his own friend, and as a dramatist. On each of these three occasions, Ben's tone varies. In 1619 he said no more to Drummond of Hawthornden (apparently on two separate occasions) than that Shakespeare "lacked art," and made the mistake about a wreck on the sea-coast of Bohemia.

In 1619, Ben spoke gruffly and briefly of Shakespeare, as to Drummond he also spoke disparagingly of Beaumont, whom he had panegyrised in an epigram in his own folio of 1616, and was again to praise in the commendatory verses in the Folio. He spoke still more harshly of Drayton, whom in 1616 he had compared to Homer, Virgil, Theocritus, and Tyræus! He told an unkind anecdote of Marston, with whom he had first quarrelled and then made friends, collaborating with him in a play; and very generously and to his great peril, sharing his imprisonment. To Drummond, Jonson merely said that he "beat Marston and took away his pistol." Of Sir John Beaumont, brother of the dramatist, Ben had written a most hyperbolical eulogy in verse; luckily for Sir John, to Drummond Ben did not speak of him. Such was Ben, in panegyric verse hyperbolical; in conversation "a despiser of others, and praiser of himself." Compare Ben's three remarks about Donne, all made to Drummond. Donne deserved hanging for breaking metre; Donne would perish for not being understood: and Donne was in some points the first of living poets.

Mr. Greenwood's effort to disable Jonson's evidence rests on

---
[205] The Shakespeare Problem Restated, p. 453.

the contradictions in his estimates of Shakespeare's poetry, in notices scattered through some thirty years. Jonson, it is argued, cannot on each occasion mean Will. He must now mean Will, now the Great Unknown, and now—both at once. Yet I have proved that Ben was the least consistent of critics, all depended on the occasion, and on his humour at the moment. This is a commonplace of literary history. The Baconians do not know it; Mr. Greenwood, if he knows it, ignores it, and bases his argument on facts which may be unknown to his readers. We have noted Ben's words of 1619, and touched on his panegyric of 1623. Thirdly, about 1630 probably, Ben wrote in his manuscript book Discourses an affectionate but critical page on Shakespeare as a man and an author. Always, in prose, and in verse, and in recorded conversation, Ben explicitly identified Shakspere (William, of Stratford) with the author of the plays usually ascribed to him. But the Baconian Judge Webb (in extreme old age), and the anti-Shakespearean Mr. Greenwood and others, choose to interpret Ben's words on the theory that, in 1623, he "had his tongue in his cheek"; that, like Odysseus, he "mingled things false with true," that they know what is true from what is false, and can undo the many knots which Ben tied in his tongue. How they succeed we shall see.

In addition to his three known mentions of Shakespeare by name (1619, 1623, 1630?), Ben certainly appears to satirise his rival at a much earlier date; especially as Pantalabus, a playwright in The Poetaster (1601), and as actor, poet, and plagiarist in an epigram, Poet-Ape, published in his collected works of 1616; but probably written as early as 1602. It is well known that in 1598 Shakespeare's company acted Ben's Every Man in His Humour. It appears that he conceived some grudge against the actors, and apparently against Shakespeare and other playwrights, for, in 1601, his Poetaster is a satire both on playwrights and on actors, whom he calls "apes." The apparent attacks on Shakespeare are just such as Ben, if angry and envious, would direct against him; while we know of no other poet-player of the period to whom they could apply. For example, in The Poetaster, Histrio, the actor, is advised to ingratiate himself with Pantalabus, "gent'man parcel-poet, his father was a man of worship, I tell thee." This is perhaps unmistakably a blow at Shakespeare, who had recently acquired for his father and himself arms, and the pleasure of writing himself "gentleman." This "parcel-poet gent'man" "pens lofty, in a new stalking style,"—he is thus an author, he "pens," and in a high style. He is called Pantalabus, from the Greek words for "to take up all," which means that, as poet, he is a plagiarist. Jonson repeats this charge in his verses called Poet-Ape—

"He takes up all, makes each man's wit his own,
And told of this, he slights it."

In a scene added to The Poetaster in 1616, the author (Ben) is advised not

"With a sad and serious verse to wound
Pantalabus, railing in his saucy jests,"

and obviously slighting the charges of plagiarism. Perhaps Ben is glancing at Shakespeare, who, if accused of plagiary by an angry rival, would merely laugh.

A reply to the Poetaster, namely Satiromastix (by Dekker and Marston?), introduces Jonson himself as babbling darkly about "Mr. Justice Shallow," and "an Innocent Moor" (Othello?). Here is question of "administering strong pills" to Jonson; then,

"What lumps of hard and indigested stuff,
Of bitter Satirism, of Arrogance,
Of Self-love, of Detraction, of a black
And stinking Insolence should we fetch up!"

This "pill" is a reply to Ben's "purge" for the poets in his Poetaster. Oh, the sad old stuff!

Referring to Jonson's Poetaster, and to Satiromastix, the counter-attack, we find a passage in the Cambridge play, The Return from Parnassus (about 1602). Burbage, the tragic actor, and Kempe, the low-comedy man of Shakespeare's company, are introduced, discussing the possible merits of Cambridge wits as playwrights. Kempe rejects them as they "smell too much of that writer Ovid, and that writer Metamorphosis..." The purpose, of course, is to laugh at the ignorance of the low-comedy man, who thinks "Metamorphosis" a writer, and does not suspect—how should he?—that Shakespeare "smells of Ovid." Kempe innocently goes on, "Why, here's our fellow" (comrade) "Shakespeare puts them all down" (all the University playwrights), "aye, and Ben Jonson too. O that Ben Jonson is a pestilent fellow, he brought up Horace" (in The Poetaster) "giving the poets a pill, but our fellow Shakespeare hath given him a purge ... "

The Cambridge author, perhaps, is thinking of the pill (not purge) which, in Satiromastix, might be administered to Jonson. The Cambridge author may have thought that Shakespeare wrote the passage on the pill which was to "fetch up" masses of Ben's insolence, self-love, arrogance, and detraction. If this be not the sequence of ideas, it is not easy to understand how or why Kempe is made to say that Shakespeare has given Jonson a purge. Stupid old nonsense! There are other more or less obscure indications of Jonson's spite, during the stage-quarrel, against Shakespeare, but the most unmistakable proof lies in his verses in "Poet-Ape." I am aware that Ben's intention here to hit at Shakespeare has been denied, for example by Mr. Collins with his usual vigour of language. But though I would fain agree with him, the object of attack can be no known person save Will. Jonson was already, in The Poetaster, using the term "Poet-Ape," for he calls the actors at large "apes."

Jonson thought so well of his rhymes that he included them in the Epigrams of his first Folio (1616). By that date, the year of Shakespeare's death, if he really loved Shakespeare, as he says, in verse and prose, Ben might have suppressed the verses. But (as Drummond noted) he preferred his jest, such as it was, to his friend; who was not, as usually understood, a man apt to resent a very blunt shaft of very obsolete wit. Like Molière, Shakespeare had outlived the charge of plagiarism, made long ago by the jealous Ben.

Poet-Ape is an actor-playwright "that would be thought our chief"—words which, by 1601, could only apply to Shakespeare; there was no rival, save Ben, near his throne. The playwright-actor, too, has now confessedly

"grown
To a little wealth and credit in the scene,"

of no other actor-playwright could this be said.

He is the author of "works" (Jonson was laughed at for calling his own plays "works"), but these works are "the frippery of wit," that is, a tissue of plagiarisms, as in the case of Pantalabus. But "told of this he slights it," as most successful authors, when accused, as they often are, of plagiarism by jealous rivals, wisely do;—so did Molière. This Poet-Ape began his career by "picking and gleaning" and "buying reversions of old plays." This means that Shakespeare did work over earlier plays which his company had acquired; or, if Shakespeare did not,—then, I presume,—Bacon did!

That, with much bad humour, is the gist of the rhymes on Poet-Ape. Ben thinks Shakespeare's "works" very larcenous, but still, the "works," as such, are those of the poet-actor. I hope it is now clear that Poet-Ape, who, like Pantalabus, "takes up all"; who has "grown to a little wealth and credit in the scene," and who "thinks himself the chief" of contemporary dramatists, can be nobody but Shakespeare. Hence it follows that the "works" of Poet-

Ape, are the works of Shakespeare. Ben admits, nay, asserts the existence of the works, says that they may reach "the after-time," but he calls them a mass of plagiarisms,—because he is in a jealous rage.

But this view does not at all suit Mr. Greenwood, for it shows Ben regarding Shakespeare as the "Ape," or Actor, and also as the "Poet" and author of the "works." Yet Ben's words mean nothing if not that an actor is the author of works which Ben accuses of plagiarism. Mr. Greenwood thinks that the epigram proves merely that "Jonson looked upon Shakspere (if, indeed, he refers to him) as one who put forward the writings of others as his own, or, in plain English, an impostor." "The work which goes in his name is, in truth, the work of somebody else."[206] Mr. Greenwood put the same interpretation on Greene's words about "Shakescene," and we showed that the interpretation was impossible. "The utmost we should be entitled to say" (if Shake-scene be meant for Shakspere) "is that Greene accuses Player Shakspere of putting forward, as his own, some work or perhaps some parts of a work, for which he was really indebted to another."[207] We proved, by quoting Greene's words, that he said nothing which could be tortured into this sense.[208] In the same way Ben's words cannot be tortured into the sense that "the work which goes in his" (Poet-Ape's) "name is, in truth, the work of somebody else."[209] Mr. Greenwood tries to find the Anti-Willian hypothesis in Greene's Groatsworth of Wit and in Ben's epigram. It is in neither.

Jonson is not accusing Shakespeare of pretending to be the author of plays written by somebody else, but of "making each man's wit his own," and the men are the other dramatists of the day. Thus the future "may judge" Shakespeare's work "to be his as well as ours."

It is "we," the living and recognised dramatists, whom Shakespeare is said to plagiarise from; so boldly that

"We, the robbed, leave rage, and pity it."

Ben does not mean that Shakespeare is publishing, as his own, whole plays by some other author, but that his works are tissues of scraps stolen from his contemporaries, from "us, the robbed." Where are to be found or heard of any works by a player-poet of 1601, the would-be chief dramatist of the day, except those

---

[206] The Shakespeare Problem Restated, p. 466.
[207] The Shakespeare Problem Restated, p. 313.
[208] Supra, p. 143.
[209] The Shakespeare Problem Restated, p. 466.

signed William Shak(&c.). There are none, and thus Ben, at this date, is identifying Will Shakspere, the actor, with the author of the Shakespearean plays, which he expects to reach posterity; "after times may judge them to be his," as after times do to this hour.

Thus Ben expresses, in accordance with his humour on each occasion, most discrepant opinions of Will's works, but he never varies from his identification of Will with the author of the plays.

The "works" of which Ben wrote so splenetically in Poet-Ape, were the works of a Playwright-Actor, who could be nobody but the actor Shakespeare, as far as Ben then knew. If later, and in altered circumstances, he wrote of the very same works in very different terms, his "utterances" are "not easily reconcilable" with each other,—whoever the real author of the works may be. If Bacon, or Mr. Greenwood's anonymous equivalent for Bacon, were the author, and if Ben came to know it, his attitudes towards the works are still as irreconcilable as ever.

Perhaps Baconians and Mr. Greenwood might say, "as long as Ben believed that the works were those of an Actor-Playwright, he thought them execrable. But when he learned that they were the works of Bacon (or of some Great One), he declared them to be more than excellent"—but not to Drummond. I am reluctant to think that Jonson was the falsest and meanest of snobs. I think that when his old rival, by his own account his dear friend, was dead, and when (1623) Ben was writing panegyric verses about the first collected edition of his plays (the Folio), then between generosity and his habitual hyperbolical manner when he was composing commendatory verses, he said,—not too much in the way of praise,—but a good deal more than he later said (1630?), in prose, and in cold blood. I am only taking Ben as I find him and as I understand him. Every step in my argument rests on well-known facts. Ben notoriously, in his many panegyric verses, wrote in a style of inflated praise. In conversation with Drummond he censured, in brief blunt phrases, the men whom, in verse, he had extolled. The Baconian who has not read all Ben's panegyrics in verse, and the whole of his conversations with Drummond, argues in ignorance.

We now come to Ben's panegyrics in the Folio of 1623. Ben heads the lines,

"TO THE MEMORY OF MY BELOVED
THE AUTHOR
MR. WILLIAM SHAKESPEARE
AND
WHAT HE HATH LEFT US."

Words cannot be more explicit. Bacon was alive (I do not

know when Mr. Greenwood's hidden genius died), and Ben goes on to speak of the Author, Shakespeare, as dead, and buried. He calls on him thus:

> "Soul of the Age!
> The applause! delight! the wonder of our Stage!
> My Shakespear rise: I will not lodge thee by
> Chaucer, or Spenser, or bid Beaumont lie
> A little further, to make thee a room:
> Thou art a monument, without a tomb,
> And art alive still, while thy book doth live,
> And we have wits to read, and praise to give."

Beaumont, by the way, died in the same year as Shakespeare, 1616, and, while Ben here names him with Chaucer, Spenser, and Shakespeare, his contemporaries have left no anecdotes, no biographical hints. In the panegyric follow the lines:

> "And though thou hadst small Latin and less Greek,
> From thence to honour thee I would not seek
> For names, but call forth thund'ring Æschylus,"

and the other glories of the Roman and Attic stage, to see and hear how Shakespeare bore comparison with all that the classic dramatists did, or that "did from their ashes come."

Jonson means, "despite your lack of Greek and Latin I would not shrink from challenging the greatest Greek and Roman tragedians to see how you bear comparison with themselves"?

Mr. Greenwood and the Baconians believe that the author of the plays abounded in Latin and Greek. In my opinion his classical scholarship must have seemed slight indeed to Ben, so learned and so vain of his learning: but this is part of a vexed question, already examined. So far, Ben's verses have brought not a hint to suggest that he does not identify the actor, his Beloved, with the author. Nothing is gained when Ben, in commendatory verses, praises "Thy Art," whereas, speaking to Drummond of Hawthornden (1619), he said that Shakespeare "wanted art." Ben is not now growling to Drummond of Hawthornden: he is writing a panegyric, and applauds Shakespeare's "well-turned and true-filed lines," adding that, "to write a living line" a man "must sweat," and "strike the second heat upon the Muses' anvil."

To produce such lines requires labour, requires conscious "art." So Shakespeare had "art," after all, despite what Ben had said to Drummond: "Shakespeare lacked art." There is no more in the matter; the "inconsistency" is that of Ben's humours on two perfectly different occasions, now grumbling to Drummond; and now writing hyperbolically in commendatory verses. But the contrast makes Mr. Greenwood exclaim, "Can anything be more astonishing and at the same time more unsatisfactory than this?"[210]

Can anything be more like Ben Jonson?

Did he know the secret of the authorship in 1619? If so, why did he say nothing about the plays of the Great Unknown (whom he called Shakespeare), save what Drummond reports, "want of art," ignorance of Bohemian geography. Or did Ben not know the secret till, say, 1623, and then heap on the very works which he had previously scouted praise for the very quality which he had said they lacked? If so, Ben was as absolutely inconsistent, as before. There is no way out of this dilemma. On neither choice are Ben's utterances "easy to reconcile one with the other," except on the ground that Ben was—Ben, and his comments varied with his varying humours and occasions. I believe that, in the commendatory verses, Ben allowed his Muse to carry him up to heights of hyperbolical praise which he never came near in cold blood. He was warmed with the heat of poetic composition and wound up to heights of eulogy, though even now he could not forget the small Latin and less Greek!

We now turn to Mr. Greenwood's views about the commendatory verses. On mature consideration I say nothing of his remarks on Ben's couplets about the bad engraved portrait.[211] They are concerned with the supposed "original bust," as represented in Dugdale's engraving of 1656. What the Baconians hope to make out of "the original bust" I am quite unable to understand.[212] Again, I leave untouched some witticisms[213] on Jonson's lines about Spenser, Chaucer, and Beaumont in their tombs—lines either suggested by, or suggestive of others by an uncertain W. Basse, "but the evidence of authorship seems somewhat doubtful. How the date is determined I do not know ... "[214] As Mr. Greenwood knows so little, and as the discussion merely adds dust to the dust, and fog to the mist of his attempt to disable Ben's evidence, I glance and pass by.

"Then follow these memorable words, which I have already discussed:

---

[210] The Shakespeare Problem Restated, p. 482.
[211] The Shakespeare Problem Restated, pp. 467, 471.
[212] See chapter IX on The Later Life of Shakespeare.
[213] Ibid., pp. 472, 474.
[214] The Shakespeare Problem Restated, p. 473.

"'And though thou hadst small Latin and less Greek ... '"[215]

In "these memorable words," every non-Baconian sees Ben's opinion about his friend's lack of scholarship. According to his own excellent Index, Mr. Greenwood has already adverted often to "these memorable words."

(1) P. 40. " ... if this testimony is to be explained away as not seriously written, then are we justified in applying the same methods of interpretation to Jonson's other utterances as published in the Folio of 1623. But I shall have more to say as to that further on."

(2) P. 88. Nothing of importance.

(3) P. 220. Quotation from Dr. Johnson. Ben, "who had no imaginable temptation to falsehood," wrote the memorable words. But Mr. Greenwood has to imagine a "temptation to falsehood,"— and he does.

p. 252(4) P. 222. "And we have recognised that Jonson's 'small Latin and less Greek' must be explained away" (a quotation from somebody).

(5) P. 225. Allusion to anecdote of "Latin (latten) spoons."

(6) Pp. 382, 383. "Some of us" (some of whom?) "have long looked upon it as axiomatic ... that Jonson's 'small Latin and less Greek,' if meant to be taken seriously, can only be applicable to Shakspere of Stratford and not to Shakespeare," that is, not to the Unknown author. Unluckily Ben, in 1623, is addressing the shade of the "sweet Swan of Avon," meaning Stratford-on-Avon.

(7) The next references in the laudable Index are to pp. 474, 475. "Then follow these memorable words, which I have already discussed:

"'And though thou hadst small Latin and less Greek,'

words which those who see how singularly inappropriate they are to the author of the Plays and Poems of Shakespeare have been at such infinite pains to explain away without impeaching the credit of the author, or assuming that he is here indulging in a little Socratic irony."

I do not want to "explain" Ben's words "away": I want to know how on earth Mr. Greenwood explains them away. My view is that Ben meant what he said, that Will, whose shade he is addressing, was no scholar (which he assuredly was not). I diligently search Mr. Greenwood's scriptures, asking How does he explain Ben's "memorable words" away? On p. 106 of The Shakespeare Problem

---
[215] Ibid., p. 474.

Restated I seem to catch a glimmer of his method. "Once let the Stratfordians" (every human and non-Baconian person of education) "admit that Jonson when he penned the words 'small Latin and less Greek' was really writing 'with his tongue in his cheek.' ... "

Once admit that vulgarism concerning a great English poet engaged on a poem of Pindaric flight, and of prophetic vision! No, we leave the admission to Mr. Greenwood and his allies.

To consider thus is to consider too seriously. The Baconians and Anti-Willians have ceased to deserve serious attention (if ever they did deserve it), and virtuous indignation, and all that kind of thing, when they ask people who care for poetry to "admit" that Ben wrote his verses "with his tongue in his cheek." Elsewhere,[216] in place of Ben's "tongue in his cheek," Mr. Greenwood prefers to suggest that Ben "is here indulging in a little Socratic irony." Socrates "with his tongue in his cheek"! Say "talking through his throat," if one may accept the evidence of the author of Raffles, as to the idioms of burglars.

To return to criticism, we are to admit that Jonson was really writing "with his tongue in his cheek," knowing that, as a fact, "Shakespeare" (the Great Unknown, the Bacon of the Baconians) "had remarkable classical attainments, and they, of course, open the door to the suggestion that the entire poem is capable of an ironical construction and esoteric interpretation."[217]

So this is Mr. Greenwood's method of "explaining away" the memorable words. He seems to conjecture that Will was not Shakespeare, not the author of the plays; that Jonson knew it; that his poem is, as a whole, addressed to Bacon, or to the Great Unknown, under his "nom de plume" of "William Shakespeare"; that the address to the "Swan of Avon" is a mere blind; and that Ben only alludes to his "Beloved," the Stratford actor, when he tells his Beloved that his Beloved has "small Latin and less Greek." All the praise is for Bacon, or the Great Unknown (Mr. Harris), the jeer is for "his Beloved, the Author, Mr. William Shakespeare, And what he hath left Us."

As far as I presume to understand this theory of the "tongue in the cheek," of the "Socratic irony," this is what Mr. Greenwood has to propose towards "explaining away" the evidence of Ben Jonson, in his famous commendatory verses. When we can see through the dust of words we find that the "esoteric interpretation" of the commendatory verses is merely a reassertion of the general theory:

---

[216] The Shakespeare Problem Restated, p. 475.
[217] The Shakespeare Problem Restated, p. 106.

a man with small Latin and less Greek could not have written the plays and poems. Therefore when Ben explicitly states that his Beloved, Mr. Shakespeare of Stratford, the Swan of Avon did write the plays, and had small Latin and less Greek, Ben meant that he did not write them, that they were written by somebody else who had plenty of Greek and Latin. It is a strange logical method! Mr. Greenwood merely reasserts his paradox, and proves it, like certain Biblical critics of more orthodoxy than sense, by aid of his private "esoteric method of interpretation." Ben, we say, about 1630, in prose and in cold blood, and in a humour of criticism without the old rancour and envy, or the transitory poetic enthusiasm, pens a note on Shakespeare in a volume styled "Timber, or Discoveries, made upon men and Matter, as they have flowed out of his daily Readings; or had their reflux to his peculiar Notion of the Times." Ben died in 1637; his MS. collection of notes and brief essays, and reflections, was published in 1641. Bacon, of whom he wrote his impressions in this manuscript, had died in 1626. Ben was no longer young: he says, among these notes, that his memory, once unusually strong, after he was past forty "is much decayed in me ... It was wont to be faithful to me, but shaken with age now..." (I copy the extract as given by Mr. Greenwood.[218]) He spoke sooth: he attributes to Orpheus, in "Timber," a line from Homer, and quotes from Homer what is not in that poet's "works."

In this manuscript occurs, then, a brief prose note, headed, De Shakespeare nostrati, on our countryman Shakespeare. It is an anecdote of the Players and their ignorance, with a few critical and personal remarks on Shakespeare. "I remember the players have often mentioned it as an honour to Shakespeare that (whatsoever he penned) he never blotted out a line. My answer hath been, 'Would he had blotted a thousand,' which they thought a malevolent speech. I had not told posterity this but for their ignorance who chose that circumstance to commend their friend by (that) wherein he most faulted; and to justify mine own candour, for I loved the man, and do honour his memory on this side idolatry as much as any. He was, indeed, honest, and of an open and free nature; had an excellent phantasy, brave notions and gentle expressions, wherein he flowed with that facility that sometimes it was necessary he should be stopped. 'Sufflaminandus erat,' as Augustus said of Haterius. His wit was in his own power; would the rule of it had been so too! Many times he fell into those things could not escape laughter, as when he said in the person of Cæsar, one speaking to him, 'Cæsar, thou dost me wrong.' He replied, 'Cæsar did never

---

[218] The Shakespeare Problem Restated, p. 478.

wrong but with just cause'; and such like, which were ridiculous. But he redeemed his vices with his virtues. There was ever more in him to be praised than to be pardoned." Baconians actually maintain that Ben is here speaking of Bacon.

Of whom is Ben writing? Of the author of Julius Cæsar,—certainly, from which, his memory failing, he misquotes a line. If Ben be in the great secret—that the author was Bacon, or Mr. Greenwood's Great Unknown, he is here no more enthusiastic about the Shadow or the Statesman, than about Shakespeare; no less cool and critical, whoever may be the subject of his comments. Whether, in the commendatory verses, he referred to the Actor-Author, or Bacon, or the Shining Shadow, or all of them at once, he is now in a mood very much more cool and critical. If to be so cool and critical is violently inconsistent in the case of the Stratford actor, it is not less so if Ben has Bacon or the Shadow in his mind. Meanwhile the person of whom he speaks is here the actor-author, whom the players, his friends, commended "wherein he faulted," namely, in not "blotting" where, in a thousand cases, Ben wishes that he had blotted. Can the most enthusiastic Baconian believe that when Ben wrote about the players' ignorant applause of Shakespeare's, of their friend's lack of care in correction, Ben had Bacon in his mind?

As for Mr. Greenwood, he says that in Ben's sentence about the players and their ignorant commendation, "we have it on Jonson's testimony that the players looked upon William Shakspere the actor as the author of the plays and praised him for never blotting out a line." We have it, and how is the critic to get over or round the fact? Thus, "We know that this statement" (about the almost blotless lines) "is ridiculous; that if the players had any unblotted manuscripts in their hands (which is by no means probable) they were merely fair copies..."

Perhaps, but the Baconians appear to assume that a "fair copy" is not, and cannot be, a copy in the handwriting of the author.

As I have said before, the Players knew Will's handwriting, if he could write. If they received his copy in a hand not his own, and were not idiots, they could not praise him and his unerring speed and accuracy in penning his thoughts. If, on the other hand, Will could not write, in their long friendship with Will, the Players must have known the fact, and could not possibly believe, as they certainly did, "on Jonson's testimony" in his authorship.

To finish Mr. Greenwood's observations, "if they" (the players) "really thought that the author of the plays wrote them off currente calamo, and never" (or "hardly ever") "blotted a line, never revised, never made any alterations, they knew nothing whatever concerning the real Shakespeare."[219]

Nothing whatever? What they did not know was merely that Will gave them fair copies in his own hand, as, before the typewriting machine was invented, authors were wont to do. Within the last fortnight I heard the error attributed to the players made by an English scholar who is foremost in his own field of learning. He and I were looking at some of Dickens's MSS. They were full of erasions and corrections. I said, "How unlike Scott!" whose first draft of his novels exactly answered to the players' description of Will's "copy." My friend said, "Browning scarcely made an erasion or change in writing his poems," and referred to Mr. Browning's MSS. for the press, of which examples were lying near us. "But Browning must have made clean copies for the press," I said: which was as new an idea to my learned friend as it was undreamed of by the Players:—if what they received from him were his clean copies.

The Players' testimony, through Jonson, cannot be destroyed by the "easy stratagem" of Mr. Greenwood.

Mr. Greenwood now nearly falls back on Bacon, though he constantly professes that he "is not the advocate of Bacon's authorship." The author was some great man, as like Bacon as one pea to another. Mr. Greenwood says that Jonson looked on the issue of the First Folio[220] "as a very special occasion." Well, it was a very special occasion; no literary occasion could be more "special." Without the Folio, badly as it is executed, we should perhaps never have had many of Shakespeare's plays. The occasion was special in the highest degree.

But, says Mr. Greenwood, "if we could only get to the back of Jonson's mind, we should find that there was some efficient cause operating to induce him to give the best possible send-off to that celebrated venture."[221]

Ben was much in the habit of giving "sendoffs" of great eloquence to poetic "ventures" now forgotten. What could "the efficient cause" be in the case of the Folio? At once Mr. Greenwood has recourse to Bacon; he cannot, do what he will, keep Bacon "out of the Memorial." Ben was with Bacon at Gorhambury, on Bacon's sixtieth birthday (January 22, 1621). Ben wrote verses about the Genius of the old house,

"Thou stand'st as if some mystery thou didst."

---

[219] The Shakespeare Problem Restated, p. 480.
[220] The Shakespeare Problem Restated, p. 483.
[221] The Shakespeare Problem Restated, p. 483.

"What was that 'mystery'?" asks Mr. Greenwood.[222] What indeed? And what has all this to do with Ben's commendatory verses for the Folio, two years later? Mr. Greenwood also surmises, as we have seen,[223] that Jonson was with Bacon, helping to translate The Advancement of Learning in June, 1623.

Let us suppose that he was: what has that to do with Ben's verses for the Folio? Does Mr. Greenwood mean to hint that Bacon was the "efficient cause operating to induce" Ben "to give the best possible send-off" to the Folio? One does not see what interest Bacon had in stimulating the enthusiasm of Ben, unless we accept Bacon as author of the plays, which Mr. Greenwood does not. If Mr. Greenwood thinks that Bacon was the author of the plays, then the facts are suitable to his belief. But if he does not,—"I hold no brief for the Baconians," he says,—how is all this passage on Ben's visits to Bacon concerned with the subject in hand?

Between the passage on some "efficient cause" "at the back of Ben's mind,"[224] and the passage on Ben's visits to Bacon in 1621–3,[225] six pages intervene, and blur the supposed connection between the "efficient cause" of Ben's verses of 1623, and his visits to Bacon in 1621–3. These intercalary pages are concerned with Ben's laudations of Bacon, by name, in his Discoveries. The first is entirely confined to praise of Bacon as an orator. Bacon is next mentioned in a Catalogue of Writers as "he who hath filled up all numbers, and performed that in our tongue which may be preferred or compared either to insolent Greece or haughty Rome," words used of Shakespeare by Jonson in the Folio verses.

Mr. Greenwood remarks that Jonson's Catalogue, to judge by the names he cites (More, Chaloner, Smith, Sir Nicholas Bacon, Sidney, Hooker, Essex, Raleigh, Savile, Sandys, and so on), suggests that "he is thinking mainly of wits and orators of his own and the preceding generation," not of poets specially. This is obvious; why should Ben name Shakespeare with More, Smith, Chaloner, Eliot, Bishop Gardiner, Egerton, Sandys, and Savile? Yet "it is remarkable that no mention should be made of the great dramatist." Where is Spenser named, or Beaumont, or Chaucer, with whom Ben ranked Shakespeare? Ben quoted of Bacon the line he wrote long before of Shakespeare as a poet, about "insolent Greece," and all this is "remarkable," and Mr. Greenwood finds it "not surprising"[226] that

---

[222] Ibid., pp. 489–490.
[223] See chapter XI, The First Folio.
[224] The Shakespeare Problem Restated, p. 483.
[225] Ibid., pp. 489–491.
[226] The Shakespeare Problem Restated, p. 486.

the Baconians dwell on the "extraordinary coincidence of expression," as if Ben were incapable of repeating a happy phrase from himself, and as if we should wonder at anything the Baconians may say or do.

Another startling coincidence is that, in Discoveries, Ben said of Shakespeare "his wit was in his own power," and wished that "the rule of it had been so too." Of Bacon, Ben wrote, "his language, where he could spare or pass by a jest, was nobly censorious." Thus Bacon had "the rule of his own wit," Bacon "could spare or pass by a jest," whereas Shakespeare apparently could not—so like were the two Dromios in this particular! Strong in these convincing arguments, the Baconians ask (not so Mr. Greenwood, he is no Baconian), "were there then two writers of whom this description was appropriate...?" Was there only one, and was it of Bacon, under the name of "Shakespeare," that Ben wrote De Shakespeare nostrati?

Read it again, substituting "Bacon" for "Shakespeare." "I remember the players," and so on, and what has Bacon to do here? "Sometimes it was necessary that Bacon should be stopped." "Many times Bacon fell into those things could not escape laughter," such as Cæsar's supposed line, "and such like, which were ridiculous." "Bacon redeemed his vices with his virtues. There was ever more in Bacon to be praised than to be pardoned."

Thus freely, according to the Baconians, speaks Ben of Bacon, whom he here styles "Shakespeare,"—Heaven knows why! while crediting him with the players as his friends. Ben could not think or speak thus of Bacon. Mr. Greenwood occupies his space with these sagacities of the Baconians; one marvels why he takes the trouble. We are asked why Ben wrote so little and that so cool ("I loved him on this side idolatry as much as any") about Shakespeare. Read through Ben's Discoveries: what has he to say about any one of his great contemporary dramatists, from Marlowe to Beaumont? He says nothing about any of them; though he had panegyrised them, as he panegyrised Beaumont, in verse. In his prose Discoveries he speaks, among English dramatists, of Shakespeare alone.

We are also asked by the Baconians to believe that his remarks on Bacon under the name of Shakespeare are really an addition to his more copious and infinitely more reverential observations on Bacon, named by his own name; "I have and do reverence him for the greatness that was only proper to himself." Also (where Bacon is spoken of as Shakespeare) "He redeemed his vices by his virtues. There was ever more in him to be praised than to be pardoned ... Sometimes it was necessary that he should be stopped ... Many times he fell into those things that could not escape laughter."

These two views of Bacon are, if you like, incongruous. The person spoken of is in both cases Bacon, say the Baconians, and Mr. Greenwood sympathetically alludes to their ideas,[227] which I cannot qualify in courteous terms. Baconians "would, of course, explain the difficulty by saying that however sphinx-like were Jonson's utterances, he had clearly distinct in his own mind two different personages, viz. Shakspere the player, and Shakespeare the real author of the plays and poems, and that if in the perplexing passage quoted from the Discoveries he appears to confound one with the other, it is because the solemn seal of secrecy had been imposed on him." They would say, they do say all that. Ben is not to let out that Bacon is the author. So he tells us of Bacon that he often made himself ridiculous, and so forth,—but he pretends that he is speaking of Shakespeare.

All this wedge of wisdom, remember, is inserted between the search for "the efficient cause" of Ben's panegyric (1623), in the Folio, on his Beloved Mr. William Shakespeare, and the discovery of Ben's visits to Bacon in 1621–3.

Does Mr. Greenwood mean that Ben, in 1623 (or earlier), knew the secret of Bacon's authorship, and, stimulated by his hospitality, applauded his works in the Folio, while, as he must not disclose the secret, he throughout speaks of Bacon as Shakespeare, puns on that name in the line about seeming "to shake a lance," and salutes the Lord of Gorhambury as "Sweet Swan of Avon"? Mr. Greenwood cannot mean that; for he is not a Baconian. What does he mean?

Put together his pages 483, 489–491. On the former we find how "it would appear" that Jonson thought the issue of the Folio (1623) "a very special occasion," and that perhaps if we could only "get to the back of his mind, we should find that there was some efficient cause operating to induce him to give the best possible send-off to that celebrated venture." Then skip to pp. 489–491, and you find very special occasions: Bacon's birthday feast with its "mystery"; Ben as one of Bacon's "good pens," in 1623. "The best of these good pens, it seems, was Jonson."[228] On what evidence does it "seem"? The opinion of Judge Webb.

Is this supposed collaboration with Bacon in 1623, "the efficient cause operating to induce" Ben "to give the best possible

---

[227] The Shakespeare Problem Restated, p. 488.
[228] The Shakespeare Problem Restated, p. 491.

send-off" to the Folio? How could this be the "efficient cause" if Bacon were not the author of the plays?

Mr. Greenwood, like the Genius at the birthday supper,

"Stands as if some mystery he did."

On a trifling point of honour, namely, as to whether Ben were a man likely to lie, tortuously, hypocritically, to be elaborately false about the authorship of the Shakespearean plays, it is hopelessly impossible to bring the Baconians and Mr. Greenwood (who "holds no brief for the Baconians") to my point of view. Mr. Greenwood rides off thus—what the Baconians do is unimportant.

"There are, as everybody knows, many falsehoods that are justifiable, some that it is actually a duty to tell." It may be so; I pray that I may never tell any of them (or any more of them).

Among justifiable lies I do not reckon that of Scott if ever he plumply denied that he wrote the Waverley novels. I do not judge Sir Walter. Heaven forbid! But if, in Mr. Greenwood's words, he, "we are told, thought it perfectly justifiable for a writer who wished to preserve his anonymity, to deny, when questioned, the authorship of a work, since the interrogator had no right to put such a question to him,"[229] I disagree with Sir Walter. Many other measures, in accordance with the conditions of each case, were open to him. Some are formulated by his own Bucklaw, in The Bride of Lammermoor, as regards questions about what occurred on his bridal night. Bucklaw would challenge the man, and cut the lady, who asked questions. But Scott's case, as cited, applies only to Bacon (or Mr. Greenwood's Unknown), if he were asked whether or not he were the author of the plays. No idiot, at that date, was likely to put the question! But, if anyone did ask, Bacon must either evade, or deny, or tell the truth.

On the parallel of Scott, Bacon could thus deny, evade, or tell the truth. But the parallel of Scott is not applicable to any other person except to the author who wishes to preserve his anonymity, and is questioned. The parallel does not apply to Ben. He had not written the Shakespearean plays. Nobody was asking him if he had written them. If he knew that the author was Bacon, and knew it under pledge of secrecy, and was asked (per impossibile) "Who wrote these plays?" he had only to say, "Look at the title-page." But no mortal was asking Ben the question. But we are to suppose that, in the panegyric and in Discoveries, Ben chooses to assert, first, that Shakespeare was his Beloved, his Sweet Swan of Avon; and that he "loved him, on this side idolatry, as much as any." There is no

---

[229] The Shakespeare Problem Restated, p. 295, cf. p. 499.

evidence that he did love Shakespeare, except his own statement, when, according to the Baconians, he is really speaking of Bacon, and, according to Mr. Greenwood, of an unknown person, singularly like Bacon. Consequently, unless we can prove that Ben really loved the actor, he is telling a disgustingly hypocritical and wholly needless falsehood, both before and after the death of Bacon. To be silent about the authorship of a book, an authorship which is the secret of your friend and patron, is one thing and a blameless thing. All the friends, some twenty, to whom Scott confided the secret of his authorship were silent. But not one of them publicly averred that the author was their very dear friend, So-and-so, who was not Scott, and perhaps not their friend at all. That was Ben's line. Thus the parallel with Scott drawn by Mr. Greenwood, twice,[230] is no parallel. It has no kind of analogy with Ben's alleged falsehoods, so elaborate, so incomprehensible except by Baconians, and, if he did not love the actor Shakspere dearly, so detestably hypocritical, and open to instant detection.

It is not easy to find a parallel to the conduct with which Ben is charged. But suppose that Scott lived unsuspected of writing his novels, which, let us say, he signed "James Hogg," and died without confessing his secret, and without taking his elaborate precautions for its preservation on record.

Next, imagine that Lockhart knew Scott's secret, under vow of silence, and was determined to keep it at any cost. He therefore, writing after the death of Hogg of Ettrick, and in Scott's lifetime, publishes verses declaring that Hogg was his "beloved" (an enormous fib), and that Hogg, "Sweet Swan of Ettrick," was the author of the Waverley novels.

To complete the parallels, Lockhart, after Scott's death, leaves a note in prose to the effect that, while he loved Hogg on this side idolatry (again, a monstrous fable), he must confess that Hogg, author of the Waverley novels, often fell into things that were ridiculous; and often needed to have a stopper put on him for all these remarks. Lockhart, while speaking of Hogg, is thinking of Scott—and he makes the remarks solely to conceal Scott's authorship of the novels—of which, on the hypothesis, nobody suspected Scott to be the author. Lockhart must then have been what the Baconian Mr. Theobald calls Mr. Churton Collins, "a measureless liar,"—all for no reason.

Mr. Greenwood, starting as usual from the case, which is no parallel, of Scott's denying his own authorship, goes on, "for all we know, Jonson might have seen nothing in the least objectionable in

---

[230] The Shakespeare Problem Restated, pp. 295, 499.

the publication by some great personage of his dramatic works under a pseudonym" (under another man's name really), "even though that pseudonym led to a wrong conception as to the authorship; and that, if, being a friend of that great personage, and working in his service" (Ben worked, by the theory, in Bacon's), "he had solemnly engaged to preserve the secret inviolate, and not to reveal it even to posterity, then doubtless ('I thank thee, Jew' (meaning Sir Sidney Lee), 'for teaching me that word'!) he would have remained true to that solemn pledge."[231]

To remain "true," Ben had only to hold his peace. But he lied up and down, and right and left, and even declared that Bacon was a friend of the players, and needed to be shut up, and made himself a laughing-stock in his plays,—styling Bacon "Shakespeare." All this, and much more of the same sort, we must steadfastly believe before we can be Baconians, for only by believing these doctrines can we get rid of Ben Jonson's testimony to the authorship of Will Shakspere, Gent.

---

[231] The Shakespeare Problem Restated, p. 499.

XIII

THE PREOCCUPATIONS OF BACON

Let us now examine a miracle and mystery in which the Baconians find nothing strange; nothing that is not perfectly normal. Bacon was the author of the Shakespearean plays, they tell us. Let us look rapidly at his biography, after which we may ask, does not his poetic supremacy, and imaginative fertility, border on the miraculous, when we consider his occupations and his ruling passion?

Bacon, born in 1561, had a prodigious genius, was well aware of it, and had his own ideal as to the task which he was born to do. While still at Cambridge, and therefore before he was fifteen, he was utterly dissatisfied, as he himself informed Dr. Rawley, with the scientific doctrines of the Schools. In the study of nature they reasoned from certain accepted ideas, a priori principles, not from what he came to call "interrogation of Nature." There were, indeed, and had long been experimental philosophers, but the school doctors went not beyond Aristotle; and discovered nothing. As Mr. Spedding puts it, the boy Bacon asked himself, "If our study of nature be thus barren, our method of study must be wrong; might not a better method be found? ... Upon the conviction 'This may be done,' followed at once the question, How may it be done? Upon that question answered followed the resolution to try and do it."

This was, in religious phrase, the Conversion of Bacon, "the event which had a greater influence than any other upon his character and future course. From that moment he had a vocation which employed and stimulated him ... an object to live for as wide as humanity, as immortal as the human race; an idea to live in vast and lofty enough to fill the soul for ever with religious and heroic aspirations."[232] The vocation, the idea, the object, were not poetical.

In addition to this ceaseless scientific preoccupation, Bacon was much concerned with the cause of reformed religion (then at stake in France, and supposed to be in danger at home), and with the good government of his native country. He could only aid that cause by the favour of Elizabeth and James; by his services in Parliament, where, despite his desire for advancement, he conscientiously opposed the Queen. He was obliged to work at such

---

[232] Letters and Life of Francis Bacon, edited by James Spedding, vol. i. p. 4 (1861).

tasks of various sorts, legal and polemical literature, as were set him by people in power. With these three great objects filling his heart, inspiring his ambition, and occupying his energies and time, we cannot easily believe, without direct external evidence, that he, or any mortal, could have leisure and detachment from his main objects (to which we may add his own advancement) sufficient to enable him to compose the works ascribed to Shakespeare.

Thus, at the age of twenty-two (1583), when, if ever, he might have penned sonnets to his mistress's eyebrow, he reports that he wrote "his first essay on the Instauration of Philosophy, which he called Temporis Partus Maximus, 'The Greatest Birth of Time,'" and "we need not doubt that between Law and Philosophy he found enough to do."[233] For the Baconians take Bacon to have been a very great lawyer (of which I am no judge), and Law is a hard mistress, rapacious of a man's hours. In 1584 he entered Parliament, but we do not hear anything very important of his occupations before 1589, when he wrote a long pamphlet, "Touching the Controversies of the Church of England."[234] He had then leisure enough; that he was not anonymously supplying the stage with plays I can neither prove nor disprove: but there is no proof that he wrote Love's Labour's Lost! By 1591–2, we learn much of him from his letter to Cecil, who never would give him a place wherein he could meditate his philosophy. He was apparently hard at scientific work. "I account my ordinary course of study and meditation to be more painful than most parts of action are." He adds, "The contemplative planet carries me away wholly," and by contemplation I conceive him to mean what he calls "vast contemplative ends." These he proceeds to describe: he does not mean the writing of Venus and Adonis (1593), nor of Lucrece (1594), nor of comedies! "I have taken all knowledge to be my province," and he recurs to his protest against the pseudo-science of his period. "If I could purge knowledge of two sorts of rovers whereof the one, with frivolous disputations, confutations, and verbosities; the other with blind experiments, and auricular traditions and impostures, hath committed so many spoils, I hope I should bring in industrious observations, grounded conclusions, and profitable inventions and discoveries ... This, whether it be curiosity, or vainglory, or nature, or (if one take it favourably) philanthropy, is so fixed in my mind that it cannot be removed." If Cecil cannot help him to a post, if he cannot serve the truth, he will reduce himself, like Anaxagoras, to voluntary poverty, " ... and

---

[233] Letters and Life of Francis Bacon, edited by James Spedding, vol. i. p. 31.
[234] Ibid., vol. i. pp. 74–95.

become some sorry bookmaker, or a true pioneer in that mine of truth ... "[235] Really, from first to last he was the prince of begging-letter writers, endlessly asking for place, pensions, reversions, money, and more money.

Though his years were thirty-one, Bacon was as young at heart as Shelley at eighteen, when he wrote thus to Cecil, "my Lord Treasurer Burghley." What did Cecil care for his youngish kinsman's philanthropy, and "vast speculative ends" (how modern it all is!), and the rest of it? But just because Bacon, at thirty-one, is so extremely "green," going to "take all knowledge for his province" (if some one will only subsidise him, and endow his research), I conceive that he was in earnest about his reformation of science. Surely no Baconian will deny it! Being so deeply in earnest, taking his "study and meditation" so hard, I cannot see him as the author of Venus and Adonis, and whatever plays of the period,—say, Love's Labour's Lost, The Two Gentlemen of Verona, Henry VI, Part I,— are attributed to him, about this time, by Baconians. Of course my view is merely personal or "subjective." The Baconians' view is also "subjective." I regard Bacon, in 1591, and later, as intellectually preoccupied by his vast speculative aims:—what he says that he desires to do, in science, is what he did, as far as he was able. His other desires, his personal advancement, money, a share in the conduct of affairs, he also hotly pursued, not much to his own or the public profit. There seems to be no room left, no inclination left, for competition in their own line with Marlowe, Greene, Nash, and half a dozen other professed playwrights: no room for plays done under the absurd pseudonym of an ignorant actor.

You see these things as the Baconians do, or as I do. Argument is unavailing. I take Bacon to have been sincere in his effusive letter to Cecil. Not so the Baconians; he concealed, they think, a vast literary aim. They must take his alternative—to be "some sorry bookmaker, or a pioneer in that mine of truth," as meaning that he would either be the literary hack of a company of players, or the founder of a regenerating philosophy. But, at that date, playwrights could not well be called "bookmakers," for the owners of the plays did their best to keep them from appearing as printed books. If Bacon by "bookmaker" meant "playwright," he put a modest value on his poetical work!

Meanwhile (1591–2), Bacon attached himself to the young, beautiful, and famous Essex, on the way to be a Favourite, and gave him much excellent advice, as he always did, and, as always, his

---

[235] Letters and Life of Francis Bacon, edited by James Spedding, vol. i. pp. 108–109.

advice was not taken. It is not a novel suggestion, that Essex is the young man to whom Bacon is so passionately attached in the Sonnets traditionally attributed to Shakespeare. "I applied myself to him" (that is, to Essex), says Bacon, "in a manner which, I think, happeneth rarely among men." The poet of the Sonnets applies himself to the Beloved Youth, in a manner which (luckily) "happeneth rarely among men."

It is difficult to fit the Sonnets into Bacon's life. But, if you pursue the context of what Bacon says concerning Essex, you find that he does not speak openly of a tenderly passionate attachment to that young man; not more than this, "I did nothing but advise and ruminate with myself, to the best of my understanding, propositions and memorials of anything that might concern his Lordship's honour, fortune, or service."[236] As Bacon did nothing but these things (1591–2), he had no great leisure for writing poetry and plays. Moreover, speaking as a poet, in the Sonnets, he might poetically exaggerate his intense amatory devotion to Essex into the symbolism of his passionate verse. Was Essex then a married man? If so, the Sonneteer's insistence on his marrying must be symbolical of—anything else you please.

We know that Bacon, at this period, "did nothing" but "ruminate" about Essex. The words are his own! (1604). No plays, no Venus and Adonis, nothing but enthusiastic service of Essex and the Sonnets. Mr. Spedding, indeed, thinks that, to adorn some pageant of Essex (November 17, 1592), Bacon kindly contributed such matter as "Mr. Bacon in Praise of Knowledge" (containing his usual views about regenerating science), and "Mr. Bacon's Discourse in Praise of his Sovereign."[237] Both are excellent, though, for a Court festival, not very gay.

He also, very early in 1593, wrote an answer to Father Parson's (?) famous indictment of Elizabeth's Government, in Observations on a Libel.[238] What with ruminating on Essex, and this essay, he was not solely devoted to Venus and Adonis and to furbishing-up old plays, though, no doubt, he may have unpacked his bosom in the Sonnets, and indulged his luscious imaginations in Venus and Adonis. I would not limit the potentialities of his genius. But, certainly, this amazing man was busy in quite other matters

---

[236] Letters and Life of Francis Bacon, edited by James Spedding, vol. i. p. 106.
[237] Ibid., vol. i. pp. 121–143.
[238] Sixty pages in Spedding's Letters and Life of Francis Bacon, vol. i. pp. 146–208.

than poetry; not to mention his severe "study and meditation" on science.

All these activities of Bacon, in the year of Venus and Adonis, do not exhaust his exercises. Bacon, living laborious days, plunged into the debate in the Commons on Supply and fell into Elizabeth's disgrace, and vainly competed with Coke for the Attorney-Generalship, and went on to write a pamphlet on the conspiracy of Lopez, and to try to gain the office of Solicitor-General, to manage Essex's affairs, to plead at the Bar, to do Crown work as a lawyer, to urge his suit for the Solicitorship; to trifle with the composition of "Formularies and Elegancies" (January 1595), to write his Essays, to try for the Mastership of the Rolls, to struggle with the affairs of the doomed Essex (1600–1), while always "labouring in secret" at that vast aim of the reorganisation of natural science, which ever preoccupied him, he says, and distracted his attention from his practice and from affairs of State.[239] Of these State affairs the projected Union with Scotland was the most onerous. He was also writing The Advancement of Learning (1605). "I do confess," he wrote to Sir Thomas Bodley, "since I was of any understanding, my mind hath in effect been absent from that I have done."[240] His mind was with his beloved Reformation of Learning: this came between him and his legal, his political labours, his pamphlet-writing, and his private schemes and suits. To this burden of Atlas the Baconians add the vamping-up of old plays for Shakespeare's company, and the inditing of new plays, poems, and the Sonnets. Even without this considerable addition to his tasks, Bacon is wonderful enough, but with it—he needs the sturdy faith of the Rationalist to accept him and his plot—to write plays under the pseudonym of "William Shakespeare."

Talk of miracles as things which do not happen! The activities of Bacon from 1591 to 1605; the strain on that man's mind and heart,—especially his heart, when we remember that he had to prosecute his passionately adored Essex to the death; all this makes it seem, to me, improbable that, as Mrs. Pott and her school of Baconians hold, he lived to be at least a hundred and six, if not much older. No wonder that he turned to tragedy, Lear, Macbeth, Othello, and saw life en noir: man delighted him not, nor woman either.

The occupations, and, even more, the scientific preoccupation of Bacon, do not make his authorship of the plays a physical impossibility. But they make it an intellectual miracle. Perhaps I

---

[239] See his statement (1603), Spedding, iii. pp. 84–87.
[240] Ibid., iii. p. 253.

may be allowed to set off this marvel against that other portent, Will Shakspere's knowledge and frequent use of terms of Law.[241] I do not pretend to understand how Will came to have them at the tip of his pen. Thus it may be argued that the Sonnets are by Bacon and no other man, because the Law is so familiar to the author, and his legal terms are always used with so nice an accuracy, that only Bacon can have been capable of these mysterious productions. (But why was Bacon so wofully inaccurate in points of scholarship and history?)

By precisely the same argument Lord Penzance proves that Bacon (not Ben, as Mr. Greenwood holds) wrote for the players the Dedication of the Folio.[242] "If it should be the case that Francis Bacon wrote the plays, he would, probably, afterwards have written the Dedication of the Folio, and the style of it" (stuffed with terms of law) "would be accounted for." Mr. Greenwood thinks that Jonson wrote the Dedication; so Ben, too, was fond of using legal terms in literature. "Legal terms abounded in all plays and poems of the period," says Sir Sidney Lee, and Mr. Greenwood pounces on the word "all."[243] However he says, "We must admit that this use of legal jargon is frequently found in lay-writers, poets, and others of the Elizabethan period—in sonnets for example, where it seems to us intolerable." Examples are given from Barnabe Barnes.[244] The lawyers all agree, however, that Shakespeare does the legal style "more natural," and more accurately than the rest. And yet I cannot even argue that, if he did use legal terms at all, he would be sure to do it pretty well.

For on this point of Will's use of legal phraseology I frankly profess myself entirely at a loss. To use it in poetry was part of the worse side of taste at that period. The lawyers with one voice declare that Will's use of it is copious and correct, and that their "mystery" is difficult, their jargon hard to master; "there is nothing so dangerous," wrote Lord Campbell, "as for one not of the craft to tamper with our freemasonry." I have not tampered with it. Perhaps a man of genius who found it interesting might have learned the technical terms more readily than lawyers deem possible. But Will, so accurate in his legal terms, is so inaccurate on many other points; for example, in civil and natural history, and in classic lore. Mr. Greenwood proves him to be totally at sea as a naturalist. On the habits of bees, for example, "his natural history of the insect is as

---

[241] The Shakespeare Problem Restated, pp. 371–406.
[242] The Bacon-Shakespeare Controversy, p. 198.
[243] The Shakespeare Problem Restated, p. 391.
[244] Ibid., pp. 408–410.

limited as it is inaccurate."²⁴⁵ Virgil, though not a Lord Avebury, was a great entomologist, compared with Will. About the cuckoo Will was recklessly misinformed. His Natural History was folklore, or was taken from that great mediæval storehouse of absurdities, the popular work of Pliny. "He went to contemporary error or antiquated fancy for his facts, not to nature," says a critic quoted by Mr. Greenwood.²⁴⁶ Was that worthy of Bacon?

All these charges against le vieux Williams (as Théophile Gautier calls our Will) I admit. But Will was no Bacon; Will had not "taken all knowledge for his province." Bacon, I hope, had not neglected Bees! Thus the problem, why is Will accurate in his legal terminology, and reckless of accuracy in quantity, in history, in classic matters, is not by me to be solved. I can only surmise that from curiosity, or for some other unknown reason, he had read law-books, or drawn information from Templars about the meaning of their jargon, and that, for once, he was technically accurate.

We have now passed in review the chief Baconian and Anti-Willian arguments against Will Shakespeare's authorship of the plays and poems. Their chief argument for Bacon is aut Diabolus, aut Franciscus, which, freely interpreted, means, "If Bacon is not the author, who the devil is?"

We reply, that man is the author (in the main) to whom the works are attributed by every voice of his own generation which mentions them, namely, the only William Shakespeare that, from 1593 to the early years of the second decade of the following century, held a prominent place in the world of the drama. His authorship is explicitly vouched for by his fellow-players, Heminge and Condell, to whom he left bequests in his will; and by his sometime rival, later friend, and always critic, Ben Jonson; Heywood, player and playwright and pamphleteer, who had been one of Henslowe's "hands," and lived into the Great Rebellion, knew the stage and authors for the stage from within, and his "mellifluous Shakespeare" is "Will," as his Beaumont was "Frank," his Marlowe "Kit," his Fletcher, "Jack." The author of Daiphantus (1604), mentioning the popularity of Hamlet, styles it "one of friendly Shakespeare's tragedies." Shakespeare, to him, was our Will clearly, a man of known and friendly character. The other authors of allusions did not need to say who their "Shakespeare" was, any more than they needed to say who Marlowe or any other poet was. We have examined the possibly unprecedented argument which

---

²⁴⁵ The Shakespeare Problem Restated, p. 425.
²⁴⁶ Ibid., p. 431.

demands that they who mention Shakespeare as the poet must, if they would enlighten us, add explicitly that he is also the actor.

"But all may have been deceived" by the long conspiracy of the astute Bacon, or the Nameless One. To believe this possible, considering the eager and suspicious jealousy and volubility of rival playwrights, is to be credulous indeed. The Baconians, representing Will almost as incapable of the use of pen and ink as "the old hermit of Prague," destroy their own case. A Will who had to make his mark, like his father, could not pose as an author even to the call-boy of his company. Mr. Greenwood's bookless Will, with some crumbs of Latin, and some power of "bumbasting out a blank verse," is a rather less impossible pretender, indeed; but why and when did the speaker of patois, the bookless one, write blank verse, from 1592 onwards, and where are his blank verses? Where are the "works" of Poet-Ape? As to the man, even Will by tradition, whatever it may be worth, he was "a handsome, well-shaped man; very good company, and of a very ready and pleasant, smooth wit." To his fellow-actors he was "so worthy a friend and fellow" (associate). To Jonson, "he was, indeed, honest, and of an open and free nature; had an excellent phantasy, brave notions, and gentle expressions, wherein he flowed so freely that sometimes it was necessary he should be stopped." If Jonson here refers, as I suppose he does, to his conversation, it had that extraordinary affluence of thoughts, each mating itself with as remarkable originality of richly figured expressions, which is so characteristic of the style of Shakespeare's plays. In this prodigality he was remote indeed from the style of the Greeks; "panting Time toils after him in vain," and even the reader, much more the listener, might say, sufflaminandus est; "he needs to have the brake put on."[247]

Such, according to unimpeachable evidence, was Will. Only despair can venture the sad suggestion that, under the name of Shakespeare, Ben is here speaking of Bacon, as "falling into those things which could not escape laughter ... which were ridiculous." But to this last poor shift and fantastic guess were the Anti-Willians and Baconians reduced.

Such was Shakespeare, according to a rival.

But it is "impossible" that a man should have known so much, especially of classical literature and courtly ways, and foreign manners and phrases, if he had no more, at most, than four or five years at a Latin school, and five or six years in that forcing-house of

---

[247] Sufflamen is the "drag" or "brake." Ben's, "it was necessary he should be stopped," is an incorrect translation.

faculty, the London of the stage, in the flush of the triumph over the Armada.

"With innumerable sorts of English books and infinite fardles of printed pamphlets this country is pestered, all shops stuffed, and every study furnished," says a contemporary.[248] If a doubter will look at the cheap and common books of that day (a play in quarto, and the Sonnets of Shakespeare, when new, were sold for fippence) in any great collection; he will not marvel that to a lover of books, poor as he might be, many were accessible. Such a man cannot be kept from books.

If the reader will look into "the translations and imitations of the classics which poured from the press ... the poems and love-pamphlets and plays of the University wits" (when these chanced to be printed), "the tracts and dialogues in the prevailing taste,"[249] he will understand the literary soil in which the genius of Shakespeare blossomed as rapidly as the flowers in "Adonis' garden." The whole literature was, to an extent which we find tedious, saturated with classical myths, anecdotes, philosophic dicta—a world of knowledge of a kind then "in widest commonalty spread," but now so much forgotten that, to Baconians and the public, such lore seems recondite learning.

The gallants who haunted the stage, and such University wits as could get the money, or had talent (like Crichton) to "dispute their way through Europe," made the Italian tour, and, notoriously, were "Italianate." They would not be chary of reminiscences of Florence, Venice, and Rome. Actors visited Denmark and Germany. No man at home was far to seek for knowledge of Elsinore, the mysterious Venetian "tranect or common ferry," the gondolas, and the Rialto. There was no lack of soldiers fresh and voluble from the foreign wars. Only dullards, or the unthinking, can be surprised by the ease with which a quick-witted man, having some knowledge of Latin, can learn to read a novel in French, Italian, or Spanish. That Shakespeare was the very reverse of a dullard, of the clod of Baconian fancy, is proved by the fact that he was thought capable of his works. For courtly manners he had the literary convention and Lyly's Court Comedies, with what he saw when playing at the Court and in the houses of the great. As to untaught nobility of manners, there came to the Court of France in 1429, from a small pig-breeding village on the marches of Lorraine, one whose manners were deemed of exquisite grace, propriety, and charm, by all who saw and heard her: of her manners and swift wit and repartee, the

---

[248] Quoted by Sir Walter Raleigh, Shakespeare, p. 65.
[249] Ibid., p. 65.

official record of her trial bears concordant evidence. Other untaught gifts she possessed, and the historic record is unimpeached as regards that child of genius, Jeanne d'Arc.

"Ne me dites jamais cette bête de mot, impossible," said Napoleon: it is indeed a stupid word where genius is concerned.

If intellectual "miracles" were impossible to genius, even Bacon could not have been and done all that he was and did, and also the author of the Shakespearean plays and poems; even Ben could not have been the scholar that he was. For the rest, I need not return on my tracks and explain once more such shallow mysteries as the "Silence of Philip Henslowe," and the lack of literary anecdotage about Shakespeare in a stupendously illiterate country town. Had Will, not Ben, visited Drummond of Hawthornden, we should have matter enough of the kind desired.

"We have the epics of Homer," people say, "what matters it whether they be by a Man, or by a Syndicate that was in business through seven centuries? We have the plays of Shakespeare, what matters it whether he, or Bacon, or X. were, in the main, the author?"

It matters to us, if we hold such doubts to be fantastic pedantries, such guesses contrary to the nature of things; while we wish to give love and praise and gratitude where they are due; to that Achæan "Father of the rest"; and to "friendly Shakespeare."

APPENDICES

APPENDIX I

"TROILUS AND CRESSIDA"

To myself Troilus and Cressida is, with Henry VI, Part I, the most mysterious among the Shakespearean plays. Here we find, if Will wrote it, or had any hand in it, the greatest poet of the modern world in touch with the heroes of the greatest poet of the ancient world; but the English author's eyes are dimmed by the mists and dust of post-Homeric perversions of the Tale of Troy. The work of perversion began, we know, in the eighth century before our era, when, by the author of the Cypria, these favourite heroes of Homer, Odysseus and Diomede, were represented as scoundrels, assassins, and cowards.

In the Prologue to the play (whosoever wrote it) we see that the writer is no scholar. He makes the Achæan fleet muster in "the port of Athens," of all places. Even Ovid gave the Homeric trysting-place, Aulis, in Bœotia. (This Prologue is not in the Folio of 1623.) Six gates hath the Englishman's Troy, and the Scæan is not one of them.

The loves of Troilus and Cressida, with Pandarus as go-between, are from the mediæval Troy books, and were wholly unknown to Homer, whose Pandarus is only notable for loosing a traitor's shaft at Menelaus, in time of truce, and for his death at the hand of Diomede. The play begins after the duel (Iliad, III) between Paris and Menelaus: in the play, not in Homer, Paris "retires hurt," as is at first reported. Hector has a special grudge against the Telamonian Aias. As in the Iliad there is a view of the Achæans, taken from the walls by Priam and Helen; so, in the play, Pandarus and Cressida review the Trojans re-entering the city. Paris turns out not to be hurt after all.

In Act i. Scene 3, the Achæans hold council, and regret the disaffection of Achilles. Here comes Ulysses' great speech on discipline, in armies, and in states, the gradations of rank and duty; commonly thought to be a leaf in Shakespeare's crown of bays. The speeches of Agamemnon and Nestor are dignified; indeed the poet treats Agamemnon much more kindly than Homer is wont to do. But the poet represents Achilles as laughing in his quarters at Patroclus's imitation of the cough and other infirmities of old

Nestor, to which Homer, naturally, never alludes. Throughout, the English poet regards Achilles with the eyes of his most infamous late Greek and ignorant mediæval detractors. The Homeric sequence of events is so far preserved that, on the day of the duel between Paris and Menelaus, comes (through Æneas) the challenge by Hector to fight any Greek in "gentle and joyous passage of arms" (Iliad, VII). As in the Iliad, the Greeks decide by lot who is to oppose Hector; but by the contrivance of Odysseus (not by chance, as in Homer) the lot falls on Aias. In the Iliad Aias is as strong and sympathetic as Porthos in Les Trois Mousquetaires. The play makes him as great an eater of beef, and as stupid as Sir Andrew Aguecheek. Achilles, save in a passage quite out of accord with the rest of the piece, is nearly as dull as Aias, is discourteous, and is cowardly! No poet and no scholar who knew Homer's heroes in Homer's Greek, could thus degrade them; and the whole of the revilings of Thersites are loathsome in their profusion of filthy thoughts. It does not follow that Will did not write the part of Thersites. Some of the most beautiful and Shakespearean pieces of verse adorn the play; one would say that no man but Will could have written them. Troilus and Cressida, at first, appear "to dally with the innocence of love"; and nothing can be nobler and more dramatic than the lines in which Cressida, compelled to go to her father, Calchas, in the Greek camp, in exchange for Antenor, professes her loyalty in love. But the Homeric and the alien later elements,—the story of false love,—cannot be successfully combined. The poet, whoever he was, appears to weary and to break down. He ends, indeed, as the Iliad ends, with the death of Hector, but Hector, in the play, is murdered, while resting unarmed, without shield and helmet, after stripping a suit of sumptuous mail from a nameless runaway. In the play he has slain Patroclus, but has not stripped him of the armour of Achilles, which, in Homer, he is wearing. Achilles then meets Hector, but far from rushing to avenge on him Patroclus, he retires like a coward, musters his men, and makes them surround and slay the defenceless Hector.

Cressida, who is sent to her father Calchas, in the Greek camp, in a day becomes "the sluttish spoil of opportunity," and of Diomede, and the comedy praised by the preface-writer of a quarto of 1609, is a squalid tragedy reeking of Thersites and Pandarus, of a light o' love, and the base victory of cruel cowardice over knightly Hector. Yet there seemed to be muffled notes from the music, and broken lights from the splendour of Homer. When Achilles eyes Hector all over, during a truce, and insultingly says that he is thinking in what part of his body he shall drive the spear, we are reminded of Iliad, XXII, 320–326, where Achilles searches his own armour, worn by Patroclus, stripped by Hector from him, and worn by Hector, for a chink in the mail. Yet, after all, these points are taken, not from the Iliad, but from Caxton's popular Troy Book.

Once more, when Hector is dead, and Achilles bids his men to

> "cry amain,
> Achilles hath the mighty Hector slain,"

we think of Iliad, XXII, 390–393, where Achilles commands the Myrmidons to go singing the pæan

"Glory have we won, we have slain great Hector!"

The sumptuous armour stripped by Hector from a nameless man, recalls his winning of the arms of Achilles from Patroclus. But, in fact, this passage is also borrowed, with the murder of Hector, from Caxton, except as regards the pæan.

It may be worth noting that Chapman's first instalment of his translation of the Iliad, containing Books I, II, and VII–XI, appeared in 1598, and thence the author could adapt the passages from Iliad, Book VII. In or about 1598–9 occurred, in Histriomastix, by Marston and others, a burlesque speech in which Troilus, addressing Cressida, speaks of "thy knight," who "Shakes his furious Speare," while in April 1599, Henslowe's account-book contains entries of money paid to Dekker and Chettle for a play on Troilus and Cressida, for the Earl of Nottingham's Company.[250] Of this play no more is known, nor can we be sure that Chapman's seven Books of the Iliad (I, II, VII–XI) of 1598 attracted the attention of playwrights, from Shakespeare to Chettle and Dekker, to Trojan affairs. The coincidences at least are curious. If "Shakes his furious Speare" in Histriomastix refers to Shakespeare in connection with Cressida, while, in 1599, Dekker and Chettle were doing a Troilus and Cressida for a company not Shakespeare's, then there were two Troilus and Cressida in the field. A licence to print a Troilus and Cressida was obtained in 1602–3, but the quarto of our play, the Shakespearean play, is of 1609, "as it is acted by my Lord Chamberlain's men," that is, by Shakespeare's Company. Now Dekker and Chettle wrote, apparently, for Lord Nottingham's Company. One quarto of 1609 declares, in a Preface, that the play has "never been staled with the stage"; another edition of the same year, from the same publishers, has not the Preface, but declares that the piece "was acted by the King's Majesty's servants at the

---

[250] The Shakespeare Problem Restated, pp. 358–362.

Globe."²⁵¹ The author of the Preface (Ben Jonson, Mr. Greenwood thinks,²⁵²) speaks only of a single author, who has written other admirable comedies. "When he is gone, and his comedies out of sale, you will scramble for them, and set up a new English Inquisition." Why? The whole affair is a puzzle. But if the author of the Preface is right about the single author of Troilus and Cressida, and if Shakespeare is alluded to in connection with Cressida, in Histriomastix (1599), then it appears to me that Shakespeare, in 1598–9, after Chapman's portion of the Iliad appeared, was author of one Troilus and Cressida, extant in 1602–3 (when its publication was barred till the publisher "got authority"), while Chettle and Dekker, in April 1599, were busy with another Troilus and Cressida, as why should they not be? In an age so lax about copyright, if their play was of their own original making, are we to suppose that there was copyright in the names of the leading persons of the piece, Troilus and Cressida?

Perhaps not: but meanwhile Mr. Greenwood cites Judge Stotsenburg's opinion²⁵³ that Henslowe's entries of April 1599 "refute the Shakespearean claim to the authorship of Troilus and Cressida," which exhibits "the collaboration of two men," as "leading commentators" hold that it does. But the learned Judge mentions as a conceivable alternative that "there were two plays on the subject with the same name," and, really, it looks as if there were! The Judge does not agree "with Webb and other gifted writers that Bacon wrote this play." So far the Court is quite with him. He goes on however, "It was, in my opinion, based on the foregoing facts, originally the production of Dekker and Chettle, added to and philosophically dressed by Francis Bacon." But, according to Mr. Greenwood, "it is admitted not only that the different writing of two authors is apparent in the Folio play, but also that 'Shakespeare' must have had at least some share in a play of Troilus and Cressida as early as the very year 1599, in the spring of which Dekker and Chettle are found engaged in writing their play of that name," on the evidence of Histriomastix.²⁵⁴ How that evidence proves that "a play of Troilus and Cressida had been published as by 'Shakespeare' about 1599," I know not. Perhaps "published" means "acted"? "And it is not unreasonable to suppose that this play" ("published as by Shakespeare") "was the one to which Henslowe alludes"—as being written in April 1599, by Dekker and Chettle.

---

[251] The Shakespeare Problem Restated, pp. 491–494.
[252] Ibid., p. 495.
[253] Ibid., pp. 358–360.
[254] The Shakespeare Problem Restated, p. 361.

If so, the play must show the hands of three, not two, men, Dekker, Chettle, and "Shakespeare," the Great Unknown, or Bacon. He collaborates with Dekker and Chettle, in a play for Lord Nottingham's men (according to Sir Sidney Lee),[255] but it is, later at least, played by Shakespeare's company; and perhaps Bacon gets none of the £4 paid[256] to Dekker and Chettle. Henslowe does not record his sale of the Dekker and Chettle play to Shakespeare's or to any company or purchaser. Without an entry of the careful Henslowe recording his receipts for the sale of the Dekker and Chettle play to any purchaser, it is not easy to see how Shakespeare's company procured the manuscript, and thus enabled him to refashion it. Perhaps no reader will fail to recognise his hand in the beautiful blank verse of many passages. I am not familiar enough with the works of Dekker and Chettle to assign to them the less desirable passages. Thersites is beastly: a Yahoo of Swift's might poison with such phrases as his the name and nature of love, loyalty, and military courage. But whatsoever Shakespeare did, he did thoroughly, and if he were weary, if man delighted him not, nor woman either, he may have written the whole piece, in which love perishes for the whim of "a daughter of the game," and the knightly Hector is butchered to sate the vanity of his cowardly Achilles. If Shakespeare read the books translated by Chapman, he must have read them in the same spirit as Keats, and was likely to find that the poetry of the Achæan could not be combined with the Ionian, Athenian, and Roman perversions, as he knew them in the mediæval books of Troy, in the English of Lydgate and Caxton. The chivalrous example of Chaucer he did not follow. Probably Will looked on the play as one of his failures. The Editor, if we can speak of an Editor, of the Folio clearly thrust the play in late, so confusedly that it is not paged, and is not mentioned in the table of the contents.

"The Grand Possessors" of the play referred to in the Preface to one of the two quartos of 1609 we may suppose to be Shakespeare's Company. In this case the owners would not permit the publication of the play if they could prevent it. The title provokes Mr. Greenwood to say, "Why these worthies should be so styled is not apparent; indeed the supposition seems not a little ridiculous."[257] Of course, if the players were the possessors, "grand" is merely a jeer, by a person advertising a successful piracy. And in regard to Tieck's conjecture that James I is alluded to as "the grand

---

[255] The Shakespeare Problem Restated, p. 360.
[256] Ibid., p. 358.
[257] The Shakespeare Problem Restated, p. 495, note I.

possessor, for whom the play was expressly written,"[258] the autocratic James was very capable of protecting himself against larcenous publishers.

APPENDIX II

CHETTLE'S SUPPOSED ALLUSION TO WILL SHAKSPERE

In discussing contemporary allusions to William Shakspere or Shakespeare (or however you spell the name), I have not relied on Chettle's remarks (in Kind-Hart's Dreame, 1592) concerning Greene's Groatsworth of Wit. Chettle speaks of it, saying, "in which a letter, written to divers play-makers, is offensively by one or two of them taken." It appears that by "one or two" Chettle means two. "With neither of them that take offence was I acquainted" (at the time when he edited the Groatsworth), "and with one of them I care not if I never be." We do not know who "the Gentlemen his Quondam acquaintance," addressed by Greene, were. They are usually supposed to have been Marlowe, Peele, and Lodge, or Nash. We do not know which of the two who take offence is the man with whom Chettle did not care to be acquainted. Of "the other," according to Chettle, "myself have seen his demeanour no less civil than he is excellent in the quality he professes" (that is, "in his profession," as we say), "besides divers of worship have reported his uprightness of dealing, which argues his honesty; and his facetious grace in writing that approves his art."

Speaking from his own observation, Chettle avers that the person of whom he speaks is civil in his demeanour, and (apparently) that he is "excellent in the quality he professes"—in his profession. Speaking on the evidence of "divers of worship," the same man is said to possess "facetious grace in writing." Had his writings been then published, Chettle, a bookish man, would have read them and formed his own opinion. Works of Lodge, Peele, and Marlowe had been published. Writing is not "the quality he professes," is not the "profession" of the man to whom Chettle

---

[258] Ibid., p. 494.

refers. On the other hand, the profession of Greene's "Quondam acquaintance" was writing, "they spend their wits in making Plays." Thus the man who wrote, but whose profession was not that of writing, does not, so far, appear to have been one of those addressed by Greene. It seems undeniable that Greene addresses gentlemen who are "playmakers," who "spend their wits in making Plays," and who are not actors; for Greene's purpose is to warn them against the rich, ungrateful actors. If Greene's friends, at the moment when he wrote, were, or if any one of them then was, by profession an actor, Greene's warning to him against actors, directed to an actor, is not, to me, intelligible. But Mr. Greenwood writes, "As I have shown, George Peele was one of the playwrights addressed by Greene, and Peele was a successful player as well as playwright, and might quite truly have been alluded to both as having 'facetious grace in writing,' and being 'excellent in the quality he professed,' that is, as a professional actor."[259]

I confess that I did not know that George Peele, M.A., of Oxford, had ever been a player, and a successful player. But one may ask,—in 1592 did George Peele "profess the quality" of an actor; was he then a professional actor, and only an occasional playwright? If so, I am not apt to believe that Greene seriously advised him not to put faith in the members of his own profession. From them, as a successful member of their profession (a profession which, as Greene complains, "exploited" dramatic authors), Peele stood in no danger. Thus I do not see how Chettle's professional actor, reported to have facetious grace in writing, can be identified with Peele. The identification seems to me impossible. Peele and Marlowe, in 1592, were literary gentlemen; Lodge, in 1592, was filibustering, though a literary man; he had not yet become a physician. In 1592, none of the three had any profession but that of literature, so far as I am aware. The man who had a special profession, and also wrote, was not one of these three; nor was he Tom Nash, a mere literary gentleman, pamphleteer and playwright.

I do not know the name of any one of the three to whom Greene addressed the Groatsworth, though the atheistic writer of tragedies seems meant, and disgracefully meant, for Marlowe. I only know that Chettle is expressing his regrets for Greene's language to some one whom he applauded as to his exercise of his profession; and who, according to "divers of worship," had also "facetious grace in writing." "Myself have seen him no less civil than he is excellent in the quality he professes"; whether or not this means that Chettle has seen his excellence in his profession, I cannot tell for certain;

---

[259] Vindicators of Shakespeare, p. 69.

but Chettle's remark is, at least, contrasted with what he gives merely from report—"the facetious grace in writing" of the man in question. His writing is not part of his profession, so he is not, in 1592 (I conceive), Lodge, Peele, Marlowe, or Nash.

Who, then, is this mysterious personage? Malone, Dyce, Steevens, Collier, Halliwell-Phillipps, Knight, Sir Sidney Lee, Messrs. Gosse and Garnett, and Mr. J. C. Collins say that he is Will Shakspere. But Mr. Fleay and Mr. Castle, whose "mind" is "legal," have pointed out that this weird being cannot be Shake-scene (or Shakspere, if Greene meant Shakspere), attacked by Greene. For Chettle says that in the Groatsworth of Wit "a letter, written to divers play-makers, is offensively by one or two of them taken." The mysterious one is, therefore, one of the playwrights addressed by Greene. Consequently all the followers of Malone, who wrote before Messrs. Fleay and Castle, are mistaken; and what Mr. Greenwood has to say about Sir Sidney Lee, J. C. Collins, and Dr. Garnett, and Mr. Gosse, in the way of moral reprobation, may be read by the curious in his pages.[260]

Meanwhile, if we take Chettle to have been a strict grammarian, by his words—"a letter, written to divers play-makers, is offensively by one or two of them taken," Will is excluded; the letter was most assuredly not written to him. But I, whose mind is not legal, am not certain that Chettle does not mean that the letter, written to divers play-makers, was by one or two makers of plays offensively taken.

This opinion seems the less improbable, as the person to whom Chettle is most apologetic excels in a quality or profession, which is contrasted with, and is not identical with, "his facetious grace in writing"—a parergon, or " bye-work," in his case. Whoever this person was, he certainly was not Marlowe, Peele, Lodge, or Nash. We must look for some other person who had a profession, and also was reported to have facetious grace in writing.

If Chettle is to be held tight to grammar, Greene referred to some one unknown, some one who wrote for the stage, but had another profession. If Chettle is not to be thus tautly construed, I confess that to myself he seems to have had Shakspere, even Will, in his mind. For Will in 1592 had "a quality which he professed," that of an actor; and also (I conceive) was reported to have " facetious grace in writing." But other gentlemen may have combined these attributes; wherefore I lay no stress on the statements of Chettle, as if they referred to our Will Shakspere.

---

[260] The Shakespeare Problem Restated, pp. 317–319.

www.ingramcontent.com/pod-product-compliance
Lightning Source LLC
Chambersburg PA
CBHW011255040426
42453CB00015B/2413